Square Dance

Revised Edition

Square Dance

Fancy Quilts from Plain Squares, Revised Edition

MARTHA THOMPSON

CREDITS

President . . . . Nancy J. Martin
CEO . . . . Daniel J. Martin
Publisher . . . . Jane Hamada
Editorial Director . . . . Mary V. Green
Managing Editor . . . . Tina Cook
Technical Editor . . . . Karen Costello Soltys
Copy Editor . . . . Durby Peterson
Design Director . . . . Stan Green
Illustrator . . . . Brian Metz
Cover Designer . . . . Regina Girard
Text Designer . . . . Jennifer Shontz
Photographer . . . . Brent Kane

That Patchwork Place® is an imprint of
Martingale & Company®.

Square Dance: Fancy Quilts from Plain Squares,
Revised Edition
© 2005 by Martha Thompson

Martingale & Company
20205 144th Avenue NE
Woodinville, WA 98072-8478 USA
www.martingale-pub.com

Printed in China
10 09 08 07 06 05   8 7 6 5 4 3 2 1

MISSION STATEMENT

Dedicated to providing quality products and service to inspire creativity.

Library of Congress Cataloging-in-Publication Data

Thompson, Martha.
  Square dance : fancy quilts from plain squares / Martha Thompson.—Rev. ed.
    p. cm.
    ISBN 1-56477-586-0
  1. Patchwork—Patterns. 2. Quilting—Patterns.
I. Title.
    TT835 .T47 2005
746 .46'041—dc22

                                    2004020681

To my best friend, Chris

Contents

Introduction 8

How to Make Old Squares Sit Up and Do New Tricks 9

New Techniques for Patchwork from Squares 11

Rocky Mountain Sparkler Blocks 14

Basic Quiltmaking Techniques 16

The Quilts 25

    Tessellating Pinwheels Place Mat 26

    Tessellating Pinwheels 31

    Tessellating Blossoms 35

    Fractured Tessellations 40

    Flutterings I 44

    Flutterings II 49

    Kissing Links 54

    Hand in Hand Wall Hanging 59

    Hand in Hand around the Commons 64

    Mountain Trails 69

    Tribble Trouble 72

For Designing Minds 77

Meet the Author 79

Introduction

*S*quare Dance was first published in 1995, and it became a popular teaching aid in quilting classes everywhere. The unique techniques it introduced enlivened traditional patchwork quilting with unusual angles and even more unusual ways of constructing them.

In 1996, I published more ingenious tricks and designs in *Start with Squares*. Many of those ideas have since found their way into classrooms and other publications, further influencing the way quilters go about making patchwork.

Both of these books have been out of print for a few years, but I continue to receive enthusiastic praise and requests for each of them. So I'm happy to combine the most popular designs from these two books into this revised edition of *Square Dance*. The quilts are new; the instructions are tried and true. I hope you will enjoy a spin with this fresh, new version of *Square Dance*.

—Martha Thompson

How to Make Old Squares Sit Up and Do New Tricks

I know a man named Pete. To be correct, he is Pete Junior, because his father's name is also Pete. As you can imagine, the two are often called Pete and Re-Pete. My friend doesn't mind too much. He knows it is better to have a corny sense of humor than none at all. When he had a son he named him—you guessed it—Pete, and he calls him Pete Again. The child says the family is replete with Petes, and anyway, the joke has petered out by now and he will definitely be the last Pete, or Pete the Last.

My friend Pete comes to mind when I'm describing the stages that I go through to make the various tessellating shapes in my *Square Dance* patchwork quilts. I begin by piecing a simple quilt of squares. Then I cut it apart and stitch the pieces back together again into a second quilt. Sometimes, I go even further and cut up the second quilt to make pieces for a third and last quilt. My quilts are pieced, repieced, and often pieced again or pieced at last.

I realize that the concept of a quilt that has been pieced and then repieced will boggle the minds of those who think we quilters are all nuts in the first place. They don't understand why we buy perfectly good fabric just to cut it up and sew it back together again. Don't even mention cutting and piecing the quilt for a second and third time. They would have you committed. Just say you're cutting squares and sewing them together. That sounds simple, and it is all that you need to do to produce any of the quilts in this book.

Let me say that another way. Every one of the quilts you see here, with its hundreds of tiny triangles, tilting trapezoids, touching tessellations, teetering transpositions, taperings, and turnings (sorry), was made merely by cutting and sewing squares of fabric.

The square is the simplest and most basic shape in patchwork. We use it all the time. Usually, we stand it up straight and tall and place other squares next to it, across from it, around it, or within it. Sometimes, we go for a little drama in our designs by setting it on point. We divide it into equilateral triangles, and things really begin to get interesting. But we almost always use the traditional 90° and 45° angles when designing with squares. They just look right that way: very solid, very well balanced, and very comforting. I like squares.

Years ago, I saw a quilt that forever altered my ideas about the proper use of squares. It was a traditional Pinwheel quilt made as a scrap quilt from hundreds of different bits of fabric. Each pinwheel had four identical arms and fit neatly right up against the next pinwheel, which also had four identical arms but in a fabric that contrasted nicely with the fabric of the first pinwheel. Another contrasting pinwheel fit snugly against it, and so on, over the whole fascinating surface of this large bed-sized quilt. It was a good example of tessellating shapes in patchwork. I just knew there must be a way to piece this exquisite patchwork quilt quickly by machine.

As I stood there studying it, an idea came to me. I thought it was so simple as to be obvious. The very talented maker of the quilt happened by at that moment and very generously responded to my inquiry by sharing exactly how she had made it. She carefully drew out a shape on a scrap of paper and handed it to me, explaining that she had made a template and used it to mark and cut four identical arms for each of the pinwheels. Then she placed the pieces on a large design wall and moved them around for days and days until she liked the arrangement. Finally, she took them down a few at a time and stitched them together.

Here is the template she used. It is a common shape in traditional patchwork designs. Trace it off the page and give it to a friend who enjoys the old techniques. Subtly imply that there might even be some great value in piecing it by hand, as our pioneer ancestors did. Then, read the rest of this book, and before she finishes her quilt, you can finish ten of your own, each more interesting and beautiful than the last. Diabolical!

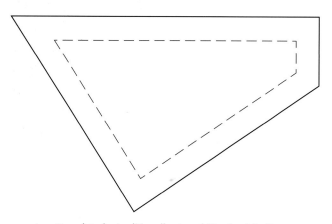

Template for traditionally pieced Pinwheel Quilt

Back to my story. I hurried home and began playing and figuring, trying things, and brainstorming with myself to figure out the secret of fast-piecing tessellating pinwheels. It wasn't so easy after all. If only I had paid more attention in high school math classes! But I kept at it, taught myself what I needed to know, and a few weeks later the answer came to me, as these little inspirations always do, in the wee small hours of the morning. I threw back the blankets and leaped from the bed. My sweet husband, who has become accustomed to such strange behavior, asked sleepily, "Another good idea, dear?" But I was already on my way to the sewing room, clutching my robe and slippers and groping around for my eyeglasses.

This book is the result of that little inspiration. All of the designs have been tested by my precious quilting friends. The quilters reported great success in following my instructions. A few even began to experiment on their own. I continue to explore and discover the zany things that happen when you take a simple square and tilt it at any odd angle other than 45°. Whirling shapes appear and dance across your quilts. And best of all, the action happens automatically as you cut and sew those humble squares, cut and sew them again, and maybe again!

New Techniques for Patchwork from Squares

My techniques for patchwork were invented especially for quilters who enjoy machine piecing and, especially, fast-piecing techniques. The designs go together quickly and with a minimum of fuss. They appear to be intricately and laboriously pieced, but the secret is that there is nothing more to the technique than cutting and sewing squares.

Beginning quilters will find the projects in this book easy enough to make with careful attention to the step-by-step instructions. Start with the sample project, then move on to one of the small quilts. Intermediate quilters will enjoy the challenge of learning a new fast-piecing technique. Advanced quilters will soon call this a no-brainer, but fun, and a great way to make scrap quilts. I hope they will be intrigued by my hints and suggestions in "For Designing Minds" on page 77.

Beginning on page 26 are detailed instructions for a small sample project: "Tessellating Pinwheels Place Mat." This project also makes a terrific doll quilt. This is the simple classroom project that I use to demonstrate how to make pinwheels from squares. The place mat can be pieced in just over an hour. I enjoy watching the lightbulbs flash on over my students' heads during the last 15 minutes of class time. Until then, they seem to accept on faith that this is really going to work.

Most of the other projects in this book are made by following the same basic steps as in the place mat. Only a simple modification or an added step or two makes a dramatic change in the overall design. If you find you're having trouble with another project in this book, refer to the basic instructions in the place mat project; the answer you need may be there.

The secret to the eye-catching designs you'll find in this book is that most of the patchwork is made using 50°, 57°, and 64° angles. They differ from the usual 45° and 90° angles that appear in most of the fast-pieced quilts that are produced today, so they gently shake the viewer awake and quietly demand attention. Your color and value choices will hold that interest through a long second look while the viewer studies the patchwork shapes more closely and begins to notice the tessellations and the movement and rhythm of the design. Finally, he or she will become intrigued by the fascinating variety of patterns in your prints, the movement set up by converging stripes, and the juxtaposition of colors—all of the elements that keep people interested in and entertained by quilts for years and years. You will have brought the viewer from a passing glance to intrigue, simply by tilting a line to a different angle.

Remember that these quilts were designed just for fun, so relax and enjoy the process. Make lovely quilts and send me pictures!

FABRIC CHOICES

Any cotton print or solid can be used in these quilts. Directional fabrics, such as stripes or plaids, work well for the pinwheels, but they are usually less successful when used in the background areas. The lines become too fragmented by the cutting and repiecing.

When mixing prints, remember to vary the scale and visual texture to keep things interesting. Mix small- and medium-scale floral prints with small- and medium-scale geometrics. Large-scale florals make fabulous borders. Mix dark and light fabrics together for maximum impact. Mix medium values or low-contrast values together for a more restful look.

Avoid placing squares of the same color next to each other when you arrange the initial grid of squares for your project, so that the pinwheels will not run into each other as you piece and repiece.

The fabric you buy is usually 42" to 44" wide. All fabric requirements for these projects are calculated on 40" of usable width after the fabric shrinks and the selvages are trimmed away. Make sure to follow the cutting instructions carefully.

THE TRACING GUIDE

Most of the quilts in this book are made with the help of a plastic tracing guide. It is not a template in the traditional sense. It is a simple square of template plastic that you cut to fit the dimensions of the project. Intersecting at the center of the square are two perpendicular lines tilted at just the right angle to produce the desired effect. The tracing guides for the "Hand in Hand" quilts are different in that they only have one line.

The size of the tracing guide and the angle of the crossed lines are tailored exactly to your patchwork. If you wish to learn how to make a custom guide for one of your own designs, refer to "For Designing Minds" on page 77. Each of the projects in this book has its own tracing guide. To be sure you are using the correct size, measure from point A to point B. Then measure the finished width of one of your grid squares. The measurements should match exactly. If not, adjust the size of your tracing guide to fit your

patchwork by making it slightly larger or smaller than the one shown.

Caution: When adjusting the size of the tracing guide, be sure to add to or subtract from it on all sides so that the intersection of the crossed lines remains in the center of the square guide.

ESSENTIAL TOOLS

You can find template plastic in your local quilt shop and in some fabric stores. It is soft enough to cut without damaging a pair of scissors or a rotary blade. It is hard enough to hold an edge even after tracing around it hundreds of times. It is translucent so you can see through it well enough to position it accurately. Wonderful stuff!

Mark on template plastic with anything that will leave a clear, dark line and not smudge or rub off. For marking fabric, most of the fabric markers on the market are just fine. Use whatever you're comfortable with as long as it leaves a clear line that you can easily see. Don't worry about whether it will wash out or disappear on its own, or even whether it might damage your fabric in fifty or one hundred years. You need to see this line only for a few minutes, through the cutting stage. You will be using the fabric marker only to mark cutting lines, not stitching or quilting lines, so it doesn't matter much what you use.

I prefer to use a permanent, black fine-tip laundry marker because it shows up so well, and I know for sure that it won't suddenly appear on the surface of my finished quilt some day, having bled out when the quilt was washed. You, however, may not feel so bold for this first project. Use something you can remove in case you mark the wrong line somewhere on the surface of your quilt.

The BiRangle® is a handy tool that is indispensable for creating the blocks in the "Flutterings" quilts on pages 44 and 49. Look for a BiRangle at your local quilt shop or order one from Martingale & Company.

TIPS FOR SUCCESSFUL OFF-GRAIN PATCHWORK

All of the little pieced blocks that go into my *Square Dance* quilts are slightly askew in relation to the lengthwise and crosswise grains of the woven fabric. Here are the important points to remember when you want to stretch the rules but not the fabric.

- Use only top-quality 100%-cotton fabrics. If the weave seems loose, try preshrinking in hot water. You may even stabilize the weave a little with spray starch or sizing—before cutting your pieces.
- Cut and handle bias edges carefully.
- Ease, but never stretch an edge to fit.
- Press very gently (never scrub with the iron), with just a little steam, on the right side of the seam. Read "Pressing Matters" on page 19.
- Allow the machine to pull the fabric through with as little help from your hands as possible. Avoid pushing it through or holding it back even a little as the machine's feed dogs attempt to pull it through.
- Adjust your machine to minimize stretching. Balance the upper and lower thread tensions. Get out your manual and learn how to do it. You'll save yourself a fortune in repairs and prolong the life of your machine.
- Use a walking foot if your machine has trouble with bias edges. My Pfaff has a built-in, even-feed feature that makes patchwork and quilting a joy. All other machines must be fitted with an attachment called a walking foot, which is usually available wherever machines are sold.
- Work with a Sharp #75/11 needle, and change the needle regularly.
- Keep feed dogs lint-free and the bobbin case oiled.

Rocky Mountain Sparkler Blocks

T wo of the new designs in this revised edition of *Square Dance* feature the Rocky Mountain Sparkler block, which uses another popular quick-piecing technique I introduced originally in *Start with Squares*. Like the *Square Dance* quilts, you start with squares, do simple piecing, and end up with dazzling quilts that no one will believe were made using shortcut techniques. They are quick to piece and almost as versatile as Log Cabin blocks when it comes to arranging them into different patterns. For practice, I recommend making the blocks one at a time. Once you feel confident, chain stitch batches of a dozen or more in an easy half hour of sewing. Here are a few design ideas from my note pages. Note that while you start with squares, the finished blocks are rectangular.

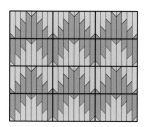

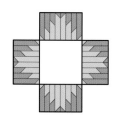

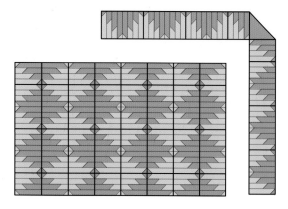

Here is how to make them.

1. Cut one square from a light fabric and one square from a dark fabric. Any size square will do, but 8½" x 8½" works well for a practice block.

2. Place the light square on top of the dark square, right sides together. Using a ruler and pencil, draw a diagonal line from corner to corner on the wrong side of the light square. Stitch ¼" from each side of the line.

3. Cut on the diagonal line. Press seams toward the dark fabric. You've made two large Twin Triangle blocks.

4. Layer two Twin Triangle blocks, right sides together, with opposite-color triangles together. Cut four equal vertical segments as shown (every 2" in this case).

 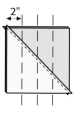

5. Rearrange and assemble the segments into a Rocky Mountain Sparkler block.

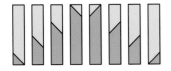 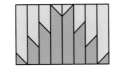

Notice that you have the look of a dark mountain silhouetted against a light sky. By simply rearranging the strips, you can have a light mountain with a dark sky.

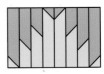 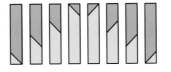

That's all there is to making Rocky Mountain Sparkler blocks. There are so many variations to this basic idea. See "For Designing Minds" on page 77 for more ideas.

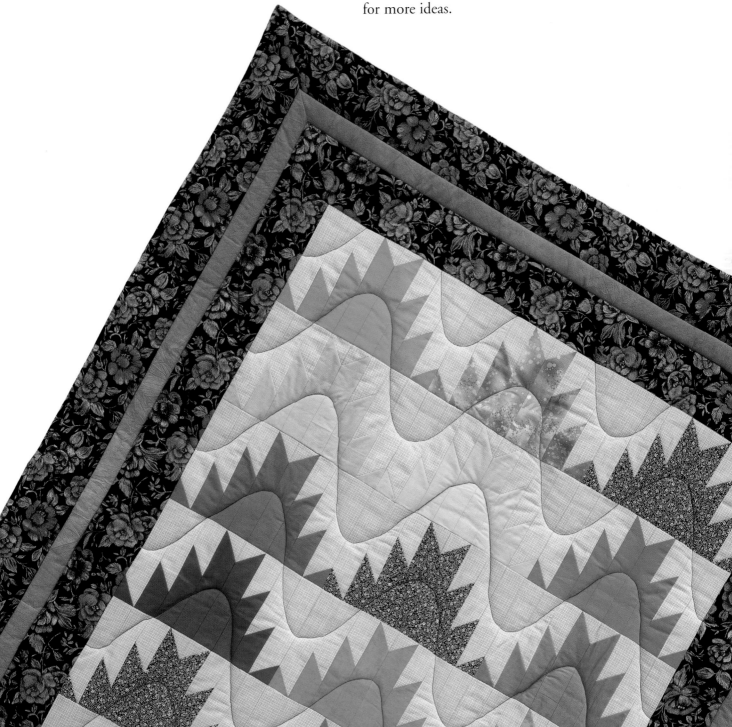

Basic Quiltmaking Techniques

Here is some basic information about sewing and quiltmaking that may be useful to you. Scan it for whatever catches your interest.

MORE THAN YOU EVER WANTED TO KNOW ABOUT GRAIN LINE

According to the rules of traditional patchwork, according to the warnings of my revered quilting teacher, and according to the strict admonitions of my fearsome high school home economics teacher (fortunately, I was paying attention in that class), the pieces around the perimeter of each block in a quilt absolutely must be on grain. The Blocks-on-Grain Rule is the first and most important rule of traditional patchwork.

Usually, I live by the Blocks-on-Grain Rule, and I teach it fervently in most of my classes. So why have I apparently flown in the face of convention and designed a slew of quadrille blocks that are (gasp!) off grain? The answer is complex, technical, and makes for pretty dry reading. You may want to skip the explanation and go straight to the "Tips for Successful Off-Grain Patchwork" on page 13. Follow these tips and you will sew any quilt in this book with ease. Continue reading for a complete explanation of how my off-grain blocks can flaunt the rules.

The grain of woven fabric is all-important to a seamstress or quiltmaker, just as the grain of wood is all-important to a carpenter. So let's review what

we mean by the word *grain*. It simply refers to the direction in which the individual threads of the fabric run. Threads that go up and down the length of the fabric are said to run on the lengthwise grain. They lie parallel to the selvage edges. They are the strongest fibers and will not stretch. Whenever possible, orient the pieces of your patchwork so that the lengthwise grain runs up and down in relation to the top and bottom of the quilt. This will maximize stability and durability. When making a large quilt, it is absolutely imperative to cut the outer borders on the lengthwise grain. If you don't, the edges of your quilt are likely to stretch and ripple, and there is no way to correct the problem. It may look all right draped over a bed, but don't try hanging it on a wall or entering it in a quilt show.

Threads that run across the width of the fabric are said to run on the crosswise grain. They lie perpendicular to the selvage edges. They are almost always weaker than the lengthwise threads and more likely to stretch a little with any kind of stress. (Aren't we all?) Small pieces on the outside edges of a patchwork block may be oriented on either the lengthwise or the crosswise grain without any problems. But, again, do not cut large pieces or long borders on the crosswise grain.

Woven fabrics have only lengthwise and crosswise threads; there are no threads that run diagonally. Cuts made on the diagonal are called *bias* cuts. When you cut a patchwork piece with none of the threads running parallel to the cut edge, you have cut the piece on the bias. The cut edge is called a bias edge and should be handled gingerly because it may stretch out of shape. When you cut a piece and all of the threads run at a 45° angle to the cut edge, you have cut your piece on the true bias. This cut edge is the weakest and most likely to stretch. Bias cutting sometimes works to your advantage in garment making, when you want fabric to drape appealingly over your curves, but it usually causes problems in patchwork. Never place a vulnerable bias edge on the outside edge of a quilt.

In patchwork, as in politics, there is always the element of bias. It can't be avoided. Understand and respect it. It can make or break the success of your project.

Now that you understand the reasons for the rules about grain and bias, I can explain why I've bent them to make my *Square Dance* quilts. To be honest, it was a matter of expediency. By cutting some pieces slightly off grain, I could move much more quickly through the piecing process than if I adhered strictly to the Blocks-on-Grain Rule. My method works because I always use good-quality (first-run) 100%-cotton fabric purchased from my local quilt shops. It works because I handle each piece carefully as I cut and sew it. It works because my stitching line functions the same way as stay stitching in garments to control stretch. Most importantly, it works for this reason: the stretchability of a bias edge diminishes significantly with every degree of change in the angle of the cut as it moves away from the true bias, or 45° angle.

In other words, a true bias edge is very stretchy, but other bias edges are less stretchy. The closer the angle of cut comes to the straight of grain, the less stretchy the cut edge will be. So, I never cut the blocks for my *Square Dance* quilts on the true bias (at a 45° angle from the grain lines). Easy.

The outside edges of the quadrille blocks are not on grain. The "off-grainness" may be technically incorrect, but there are some nice advantages to off-grain cutting. Edges don't ravel because none of the threads are parallel to the cut edge. Corners always match because bias edges ease in so readily. Stripes and directional patterns appear at unusual and interesting angles. And, surprisingly, fabrics cut on the bias contribute greatly to the "cuddleability" of a quilt by softening the hand and making the quilt a little more drapable. Try it on a baby quilt. Don't worry about a bed-sized quilt losing its shape. Borders and setting blocks are always cut on grain, and the backing is always on grain, so your quilt will remain square and hang straight. It will just feel slightly less stiff.

If you've read through all of this information in spite of my warning (and I knew you would), you now know more than you ever wanted to know about grain line. Please review the "Tips for Successful Off-Grain Patchwork" on page 13. They answer the questions on the tip of your tongue about working with off-grain blocks.

EASY CHAIN PIECING

Chain piecing is the greatest sewing shortcut of all time. If you're not already doing it, you really should learn how it's done. It speeds up your work by eliminating wasted motions. It gets you through the tedious sewing of hundreds of short, repetitive seams in minimal time. It can free your mind to wander pleasantly while your hands remain busy at the sewing machine.

Arrange the pieces to be sewn together in the proper sewing order. For the quilts in this book, you will start with a grid of squares. For example, the introductory project, "Tessellating Pinwheels Place Mat" on page

26, calls for a grid of 12 squares laid out 4 across and 3 down.

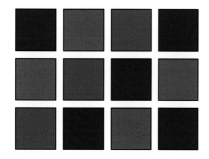

Visually separate horizontal rows by leaving a little space between them. Isolate pairs of squares within each row by leaving a little space between them also. They remind me of open books with the left and right pages facing up.

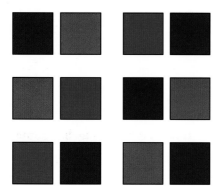

Pick up the right square of a pair and place it face down over the left square, as if closing the back cover of a book after reading the last page. Repeat for each pair of squares. Do not rotate or move the squares in any way, except perhaps to slide them to within arm's reach just to the left of your sewing machine. Keep them in order.

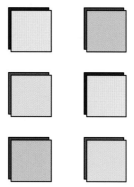

Pick up one pair of squares at a time, being careful not to rotate or flip it over. I like to start with the pair at the lower right (1) because it is the handiest, and because by stitching it first, I can get it out of the way so I won't accidentally disturb it while reaching for the ones that are farther away. Place the right edge under the presser foot. Stitch an accurate ¼" seam from the top to the bottom of the right edge.

Now, just leave it alone; don't lift the presser foot; don't remove it from the machine; don't cut the thread. Pick up the next pair of squares (2) and feed it through the machine as you did the first one. Continue picking up and sewing pairs in order (3–6) until they are all sewn. Then you may lift the presser foot, clip the threads, and remove them from the machine.

One at a time and in reverse order, clip the threads that join the pairs to release them from the chain. Replace the squares on the table in the same order as they were before stitching. To do this, you must reverse the order in which you picked them up prior to stitching. The last pair sewn (6) came from the upper left, so release it from the chain by clipping threads and place it at the upper left. Release and replace one pair of blocks at a time. The first pair sewn (1) came from the lower right, so place it at the lower right. The line of stitches should still be at the right side of each pair because you have been careful not to rotate or flip anything.

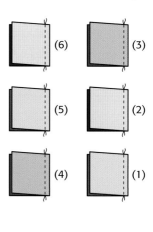

Open the pairs and lay them side by side. Look them over carefully to ensure that every square is in order and none have been rotated, flipped over, or wrongly placed.

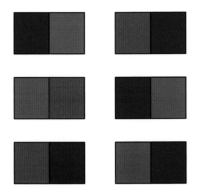

The next step is to pick up the open pair of squares at the lower right and flip it face down over its neighbor to the left. Repeat with all of the pairs. Remember not to rotate or change the positions of pieces in any way, except to slide them closer to the sewing machine. Now, pick them up one at a time and feed them through the machine in a chain as before. Remove them from the machine, clip threads, lay them in order on the table, and open them. Examine them carefully to ensure that everything is in the right place. The horizontal rows for this small project are complete. To make a larger grid with many more squares, continue sewing pieces together in the same way until the horizontal rows are complete.

Press the seams in opposite directions from one horizontal row to the next.

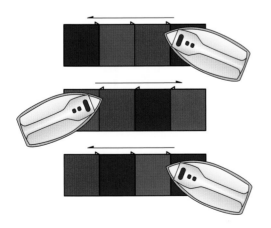

Next, stitch the rows together. Notice that when you place two rows right sides together in preparation for stitching, the seams do not conflict with one another. Rather, they lay in opposite directions, and you can feel their little ridges butt up against each other. There is no need to pin long seams in place before stitching. Simply use your fingers to pinch the edges together at each approaching intersection. Move the two pieces between your fingers slightly until you feel the ridges stop against each other. Stitch to that point; then move your fingers down to position the next seam intersection.

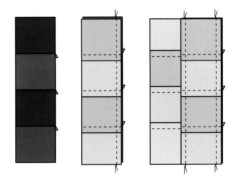

Finally, press the two long horizontal seams in either direction, up or down—it doesn't matter. Give the entire piece a good pressing with steam.

PRESSING MATTERS

Your mother probably taught you to iron, but I'd like to teach you how to press. It makes such a difference in your patchwork. Everyone who has dabbled in fast machine-piecing techniques has been introduced to one of the several good methods for piecing a grid of squares together. I've tried them all, and I always return to the method I first learned from Mary Ellen

Hopkins. So, if your habits are not yet set in stone, try it her way.

Careful pressing is as important as careful cutting and stitching in patchwork, so pay attention! Off-grain piecing requires extra care in pressing seams to avoid stretching vulnerable bias edges. Here are some good pressing techniques that will improve your patchwork, regardless of grain line.

• Press with a dry iron (no steam), or with just a hint of steam, during the initial construction of any patchwork piece. Increase the amount of steam for the final pressing of a block or section. Use maximum steam for only the final pressing of the whole quilt top just before you layer it for quilting.

• Always press a seam before crossing it with another seam. This is a hard-and-fast rule for pressing patchwork.

• Patchwork seams are almost always pressed to one side or the other; they are rarely pressed open as in dressmaking. Whenever possible, press intersecting seams in opposite directions to minimize bulk.

• Alternate the direction of seams in horizontal rows. For example, in each project, you should press all seams in the top row to the left, all seams in the next row to the right, all seams in the next row to the left, and so on.

• Always press on the right side to avoid those micropleats and minitucks that throw off the accuracy of your patchwork. Use your left hand on the underside of the patchwork to gently guide seams to the left. Hold the iron in your right hand and work slowly from right to left across the top of the patchwork, one seam at a time. Keep your left hand moving just ahead of the iron. This will take a little practice to master, but it works so well, you must try it.

• Use the left edge of the iron to brush lightly over the seam first. When you know the seam is turned the right way, use the hot bottom of the iron to press it flat. Move the iron against the seam ridge to make it lie as flat as possible. Press; don't scrub!

• Press seam allowances toward the darker fabric whenever possible.

BORDERS

Quilt borders serve multiple functions: some aesthetic, some practical. They serve as the visual frame for the composition, like the frame on a painting. They extend the size of the quilt to the necessary dimensions. They help us to "square up" a quilt. Most importantly, though, borders give us our last and best opportunity to stabilize and control the stretching of any off-grain pieces. In quilts like these, where everything is slightly off grain, a sturdy border is a necessity.

Therefore, always cut final borders for large quilts on the lengthwise grain. See the discussion of grain line on page 16. Then follow these procedures for adding borders.

Borders with Butted Corners

1. Measure the width of the quilt top across the center. Cut two border strips to that measurement. Mark the centers of the quilt top and the border strips. Pin the borders to the top and bottom of the quilt top, matching the center marks and ends, and easing (never stretching) as necessary. Sew the border strips in place. Press the seams toward the border.

2. Measure the length of the quilt through the center, including the top and bottom borders you just added. Cut two border strips to that measurement, piecing as necessary; mark the center of the quilt top and the border strips. Pin the border strips to the sides of the quilt top, matching the center marks and ends, and easing as necessary. Sew the border strips in place. Press the seams toward the border.

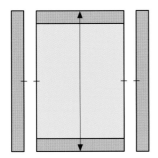

Borders with Mitered Corners

1. Cut border strips to the finished outside length and width of your quilt (including the width of two borders) plus at least ½" for seam allowances and 2" to 3" extra.

   Note: If your quilt is to have multiple borders, sew the individual strips together, matching the center points, and treat the resulting unit as a single border strip. This makes mitering corners easier and more accurate.

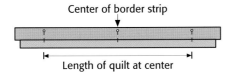

Center of border strip

Length of quilt at center

2. Mark the centers of the quilt-top sides and the centers of the border strips in the seam allowances. Stitch the border strips to the quilt with a ¼"-wide seam, matching the center marks; the border strip should extend the same distance beyond each end of the quilt. Start and stop your stitching ¼" from the corners of the quilt. Press the seams toward the border.

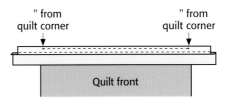

" from quilt corner   " from quilt corner

Quilt front

3. Place a corner of the quilt top on the ironing board. Fold under the top border strip so that it forms a 45° angle with the side border strip. Press and pin.

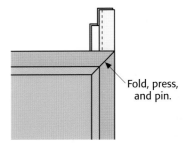

Fold, press, and pin.

4. Fold the quilt with right sides together, lining up the edges of the border strips. If necessary, use a ruler to draw a pencil line on the pressed crease to make the line more visible. Stitch on the crease, sewing from the corner to the outside edge.

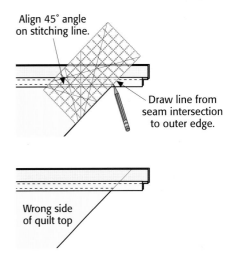

Align 45° angle on stitching line.

Draw line from seam intersection to outer edge.

Wrong side of quilt top

5. Press the seam open and trim away the excess fabric, leaving a ¼"-wide seam allowance.

6. Repeat with the remaining corners.

FINISHING THE QUILT

You probably have your favorite methods for finishing your quilts, but if you need a little guidance, the steps below can help you with layering and basting, quilting, and binding your projects.

Layering and Basting

1. Spread the backing, wrong side up, on a flat, clean surface. Anchor it with pins or masking tape. Be careful not to stretch the backing out of shape.

2. Spread the batting over the backing, smoothing out any wrinkles. I suggest using a thin polyester or cotton batting for designs with interesting geometric shapes such as these. With puffier battings, the points get lost in the thickness, and interesting quilting lines don't show up very well.

3. Spread out the pressed quilt top, right side up, on the batting. Smooth out any wrinkles and make sure the edges of the quilt top are parallel to the edges of the backing.

4. Baste the layers together with needle and thread, starting in the center and working outward. Baste in a grid of horizontal and vertical lines 6" to 8" apart. Finish by basting around the edges.

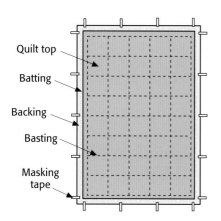

Note: For machine quilting, baste the layers with #2 rustproof safety pins. Place pins about 6" to 8" apart, away from the areas you intend to quilt.

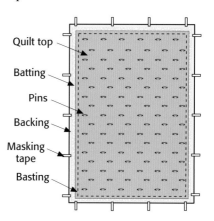

Quilting

You will find quilting suggestions for each project in this book. Most designs are suitable for both hand and machine quilting. I prefer machine quilting at this busy time of my life, and much of my quilting is done with long, continuous lines that often pass right through thick seams.

Binding

1. Trim the batting and backing even with the quilt-top edges.

2. For straight-grain binding strips, cut 2½"-wide strips across the width of the fabric. Cut enough strips to go around the perimeter of the quilt, plus 10" to allow for seams and mitered corners.

3. Sew strips end to end with diagonal seams, to make one long piece of binding. Trim the excess fabric and press the seam allowance open.

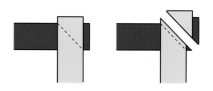

Joining Straight-Grain Strips

4. Fold the binding strip in half lengthwise, wrong sides together, and press.

5. Turn under ¼" at one end of the strip and press. Turning the end under at a 45° angle distributes the bulk so you won't have a lump where the ends of the binding meet.

6. Stitch the binding to the quilt, using a ¼"-wide seam allowance and keeping the raw edges of the binding even with the quilt-top edge. End the stitching ¼" from the corner of the quilt and backstitch. Clip the thread.

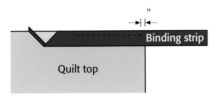

7. Turn the quilt and fold the binding up, away from the quilt.

8. Fold the binding back down onto itself, parallel with the edge of the quilt top. Begin stitching at the corner, backstitching to secure.

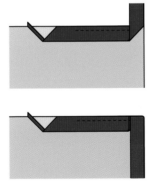

9. Repeat at the remaining corners. When you reach the beginning of the binding, overlap the beginning stitches by about 1" and cut away the excess binding, trimming the end at a 45° angle. Tuck the end of the binding into the fold and finish the seam as shown.

10. Fold the binding over the raw edges of the quilt to the back and blindstitch it in place, with the folded edge covering the row of machine stitching. A "miter" will form at each corner. Blindstitch the mitered corners in place.

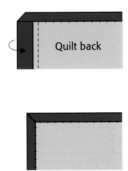

Labeling Your Finished Quilt

There must be at least 100 good reasons for labeling a quilt. If you can think of just one of them, that is reason enough to take the time to do it. At least take your permanent fabric marking pen in hand and carefully write the basics on a corner of the backing: your name, the name you may have given the quilt, the date you finished it, and where it was made. A separate label that is stitched onto the back of the quilt looks nice and can include as many details as you wish. Your label is an expression of your own personal style, so decorate it with paint or embroidery as you wish.

The Quilts

Tessellating Pinwheels
Place Mat

Finished Size: 17¼" x 14½"

Follow the instructions below to make a single place mat or a set of four. Most of the quilts in this book follow steps 1–5 of these place mat instructions. Once you've mastered a place mat, you have the skills to make a larger quilt.

MATERIALS

Yardages are based on 42"-wide fabric.

⅛ yard *each* of coordinating red, blue, and green prints for pinwheels

⅓ yard of multicolored print for background and borders

¼ yard of green print for binding

½ yard of backing fabric

17" x 20" piece of batting

Template plastic

Fine-point permanent marker (for template plastic)

Fine-point fabric marker

CUTTING

All strips are cut across the width of the fabric unless otherwise noted.

From *each* of the red, blue, and green prints, cut:

4 squares, 4½" x 4½" (12 squares total)

From the multicolored print, cut:

2 background strips, 2¾" x 42"

2 border strips, 3" x 42"

From the green print, cut:

2 binding strips, 2½" x 42"

PIECING THE PATCHWORK GRID

1. Arrange the 12 squares into a grid, 4 squares across and 3 squares down. Stand back to see if you like the way they look. Now is the time to rearrange to your heart's content. Be sure every fabric looks good with its neighbors because the sequence of colors you see will remain the same as you cut and repiece.

2. Stitch the grid of squares together. Use your favorite speed-piecing technique. If you're new to speed piecing, refer to the section on "Easy Chain Piecing" on page 17. Strive for accurate ¼"-wide seam allowances. Press the seam allowances as you go in opposite directions from row to row. Refer to "Pressing Matters" on page 19.

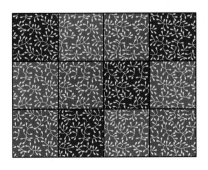

ADDING THE BACKGROUND STRIPS

The background strips allow the outside pinwheels to keep all four of their arms and float on a uniform background. Without these strips, the two outer arms of each perimeter pinwheel would be cut off.

1. Cut the 2¾"-wide background strips in half crosswise. Sew one segment to each short side of the patchwork. Trim to fit and press the seam allowances toward the border strips.

2. Stitch the remaining background-strip segments to the long sides of the patchwork; trim and press in the same manner.

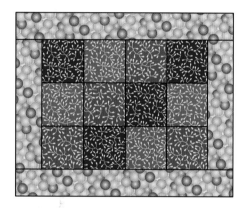

MAKING THE TRACING GUIDE

1. Place a piece of template plastic over the drawing of the tracing guide on page 30.

2. Using the fine-point permanent marker, trace the four perimeter lines and the two crossed lines onto the plastic. Write "This side up" or at least the word "Up" on the top side of the guide.

3. Cut out the guide on the perimeter lines.

MARKING AND CUTTING

1. Lay the patchwork grid on your table right side up.

2. Place the plastic tracing guide anywhere on the grid. I like to start somewhere near the center. Move the guide around until the intersection of the two crossed lines (the center of the guide) is directly over the intersection of any two seams. Twist the guide until the crossed lines lie directly over the seam lines.

3. Use a fine-point fabric marker to trace the square shape of the tracing guide onto the fabric.

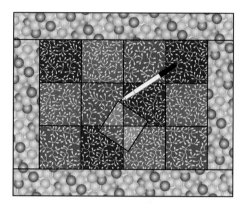

Mark the outline of the tracing guide on the grid of squares.

4. Move the tracing guide to another seam intersection. Position and trace around it as before. Continue moving, positioning, and tracing until the whole surface of your patchwork (including the background-strip area) is covered with these jaunty little squares. I like to call them "quadrilles" or "quadrille blocks," because (with the exception of the background blocks) each one is made up of four of the same-shape pieces that seem to spin around the center like a group of square dancers.

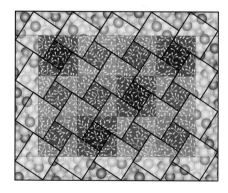

5. Cut on every drawn line with a pair of sharp scissors, thus releasing the pieced quadrille blocks. Keep them in order as you cut each one free.

CHECKPOINT

Ideally, all of the squares will fit snugly against one another as you position the guide and trace around it on the fabric. However, this will happen only if you have measured, cut, sewn, and pressed perfectly, a level of accomplishment I have yet to achieve. Instead, you may find that your squares are not consistently large enough to touch one another, or that they are too large and their lines slightly overlap a little too often.

The easy solution is to make a new tracing guide that is slightly smaller or larger as needed, and retrace *all* the squares before cutting them out. (See "The Tracing Guide" on page 12.)

MAKING THE SECOND PATCHWORK GRID

1. Rotate the blocks counterclockwise (to the left) just a little (33°, to be exact) to make them stand up straight. Keep them in order so that each pinwheel will have four identical arms once the blocks are sewn together.

2. Place the 20 blocks close together in a grid of 5 across and 4 down. (Don't worry if they get mixed up. You can easily put them back in order; it's just like assembling a child's puzzle!)

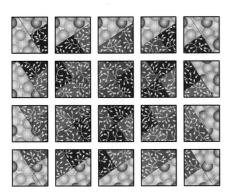

3. Stitch together the new grid of 20 quadrille blocks. Use your favorite speed-piecing technique or refer to "Easy Chain Piecing" on page 17. Strive for accurate ¼"-wide seam allowances.

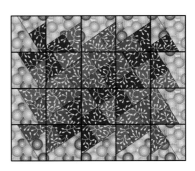

ADDING THE BORDER

Referring to the information on "Borders with Butted Corners" on page 20, cut the 3"-wide border strips in half crosswise, and then sew the segments to your place mat and trim to fit.

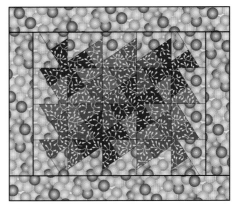

Quilt Plan

FINISHING THE PLACE MAT

Your place mat is now ready for layering and quilting. See the information on "Finishing the Quilt" on page 22. A small piece like this place mat is perfect for simple quilting in the ditch or stitching ¼" away from the seams.

After quilting, bind your place mat and enjoy it. That's all there is to it. If you can do this project, you can do any of the others in the book, so try another one and have fun with it!

SAVE THE LEFTOVERS

Notice that the number of blocks in your grid has grown and changed from the original 12 plain squares to the current 20 quadrille blocks. The background strips are now part of the perimeter blocks. Notice that as you cut the quadrille blocks from the original grid, a handful of small squares was also released. I call these "spacers." Set them aside—they are no longer needed—but don't throw them away. They are great for borders, small quilts to go with your big ones, doll quilts, or even miniatures. We quilters never waste anything!

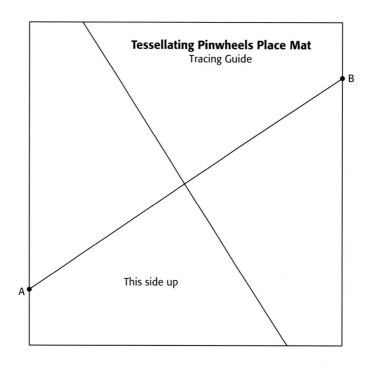

Tessellating Pinwheels Place Mat
Tracing Guide

B

A

This side up

Tessellating Pinwheels

Finished Size: 44" x 44"

Hand-dyed fabrics combine well with a juvenile theme print such as the one I chose that features budding young artists at work. Piece a grid of 49 squares; then cut and repiece a quilt of rollicking, jostling pinwheels. Cut the leftover spacer squares in half diagonally and slip them into the binding seam like fluttering prairie points to add to the carefree feel of the quilt. This pinwheel patchwork is the basis for "Tessellating Blossoms" and "Fractured Tessellations."

MATERIALS

Yardages are based on 42"-wide fabric.

1½ yards of light theme print for background and borders

1¼ yards total of assorted bright mottled prints for pinwheels and binding

3 yards of backing fabric

48" x 48" piece of batting

Template plastic

Fine-point permanent marker (for template plastic)

Fine-point fabric marker

CUTTING

All strips are cut across the width of the fabric unless otherwise noted.

From the assorted bright mottled prints, cut:

49 squares, 6" x 6"

28 binding strips, 2½" x 8"

From the light theme print, cut on the *lengthwise* grain:

4 background strips, 3½" x length of fabric

4 border strips, 4½" x length of fabric

PIECING THE QUILT TOP

1. Arrange the 49 squares into a grid, 7 squares across and 7 squares down. Sew them together, referring to "Easy Chain Piecing" on page 17.

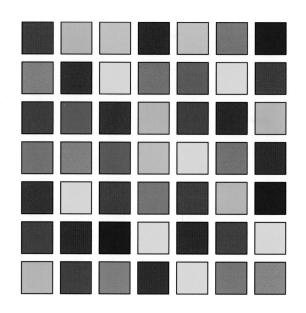

2. Stitch 3½"-wide light strips to the top and bottom edges of the patchwork. Trim to fit and press the seam allowances toward the edges. Stitch

✳ Do not press quadrille block ε once they are cut.

3½"-wide light strips to the remaining sides of the patchwork. Trim to fit and press as before.

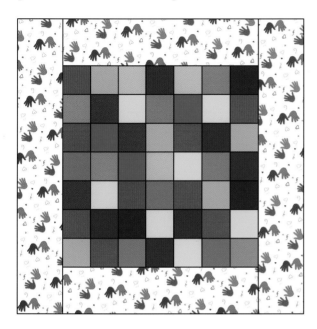

3. Make a plastic tracing guide by tracing all lines and notations from the guide on page 34 onto template plastic. Make sure that the length of line AB is the same as the finished width of your blocks and adjust, if necessary, before you cut it out.

4. Use the tracing guide to mark and cut 64 prepieced quadrille blocks. Keep them in order. Set aside the little spacer squares to use for the optional fluttering prairie points.

5. Rotate and arrange the blocks into a new grid of 64 blocks, 8 across and 8 down. Chain piece the blocks together.

6. Measure the width of the quilt top across the center and trim two of the 4½"-wide light strips to fit. Sew the strips to the top and bottom of the quilt top. Press the seam allowances toward the borders.

7. Measure the length of the quilt top, including the top and bottom borders, and trim the remaining

4½"-wide light strips to fit. Sew them to the sides of the quilt top and press in the same manner.

Quilt Plan

FINISHING THE QUILT

Refer to "Finishing the Quilt" on page 22 to layer, baste, quilt, bind, and label your "Tessellating Pinwheels" quilt. To make the scrappy binding and raw-edge prairie points, follow the steps below.

1. Join the short strips of bright prints end to end, as described on page 22 for joining binding, to make one long binding strip.

2. Use the leftover spacer squares from the patchwork to make the optional raw-edge triangle trim just inside the binding edge. Cut the squares in half diagonally, lay them along the outer edge of the quilted project, and baste in place before adding the binding. I placed mine with the long edge of the triangles flush with the outer edges of the quilt. I placed them only in the corners and overlapped their edges.

3. Attach the multicolored binding in the same manner as the plain binding to complete the quilt.

QUILTING SUGGESTION

Follow some of the seams and skip across some of the spaces to make diamonds and stars. Or, try this: use a theme print for the quilt backing and quilt your project from the back side, following the shapes in the fabric design. In the quilt shown, I quilted around playful cartoon shapes of boys and girls to coordinate with the child's theme print used in the quilt border.

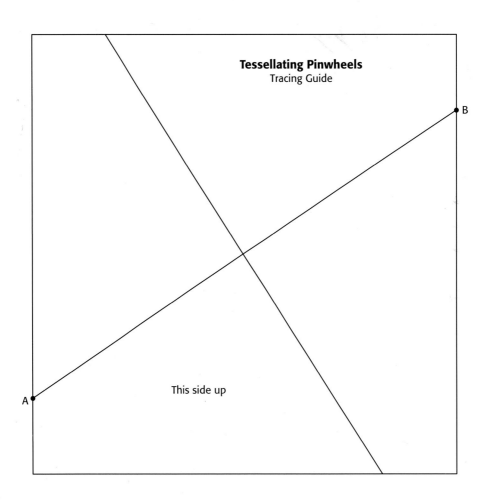

Tessellating Pinwheels
Tracing Guide

B

A

This side up

Tessellating Blossoms

Finished Size: 33" x 33"

Cutting and sewing squares is all that it takes to create these tessellating shapes. Flower blossoms jostling for space in the sunshine look great on any background, dark or light. Simply make a "Tessellating Pinwheels" quilt using the materials list given here. Then cut it up and repiece it as described on the following pages to achieve this field of colorful flowers.

MATERIALS

Yardages are based on 42"-wide fabric.

1⅝ yards of black polka-dot print for background, borders, and binding

1¼ yards total of bright hand-dyed or mottled prints for pinwheels

¼ yard of white solid for contrasting border

1⅛ yards of backing fabric

37" x 37" piece of batting

Template plastic

Fine-point permanent marker (for template plastic)

Fine-point fabric marker

CUTTING

All strips are cut across the width of the fabric unless otherwise noted.

From the bright prints, cut:

49 squares, 6" x 6"

From the black polka-dot print, cut:

4 binding strips, 2½" x 42"

From the remaining black polka-dot print, cut on the *lengthwise* grain:

4 background strips, 3½" x length of fabric

4 inner-border strips, 2¾" x length of fabric

4 outer-border strips, 2¼" x length of fabric

From the white solid, cut:

4 strips, 1¼" x 42"

PIECING THE QUILT TOP

1. Arrange the 49 squares into a grid, 7 squares across and 7 squares down. Sew them together, referring to "Easy Chain Piecing" on page 17.

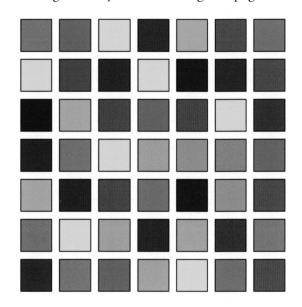

2. Stitch 3½"-wide polka-dot strips to the top and bottom edges of the patchwork. Trim to fit and press the seam allowances toward the edges. Stitch 3½"-wide polka-dot strips to the

remaining sides of the patchwork. Trim to fit and press as before.

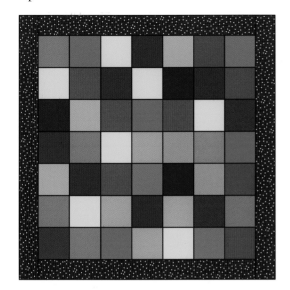

3. Make a plastic tracing guide by tracing all lines and notations from the pattern for "Tessellating Pinwheels" on page 34 onto template plastic. Make sure that the length of line AB is the same as the finished width of your blocks and adjust it, if necessary, before you cut it out.

4. Use the tracing guide to mark and cut 64 prepieced quadrille blocks. Keep them in order. Set aside the little spacer squares to use for another project.

5. Rotate and arrange the blocks into a new grid of 64 blocks, 8 across and 8 down. Stitch the blocks together, referring to "Easy Chain Piecing."

6. Use the 2¾"-wide polka-dot strips to border the patchwork. Measure the grid and trim the borders to fit the sides of the patchwork. Then measure again and trim the remaining 2¾"-wide polka-dot strips to fit the top and bottom edges of the patchwork. Press the seam allowances toward the outer edges.

7. Make a smaller tracing guide, using the pattern for "Tessellating Blossoms" on page 39. Line AB on the tracing guide should measure exactly the same as the width across your finished Pinwheel blocks, from seam to seam. If it does not, make your tracing guide smaller or larger, adding or subtracting equal amounts on all sides.

8. Use the smaller tracing guide to mark and cut 81 prepieced Flower Blossom blocks. Keep them in order. Set aside the small, pieced spacer squares to use in the "Bonus Miniature Quilt," shown on page 39.

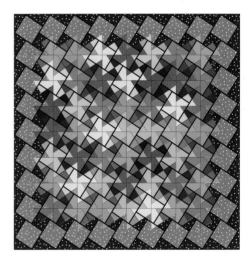

9. Rotate and arrange the blocks into a new grid of 81 blocks, 9 across and 9 down. Chain piece the blocks together.

   Note: Check the position of each seam carefully before stitching. You may have to shift blocks ever so slightly to ensure that the tip of each flower petal fits on smoothly.

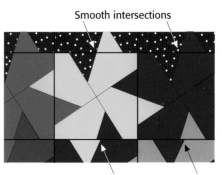

Smooth intersections

Jagged intersections

10. For a double final border, sew each of the 1¼"-wide white strips to a 2¼"-wide black polka-dot strip. Referring to "Borders with Mitered Corners" on page 21, measure the quilt top, add the border strips with the white fabric adjoining the quilt top, and miter the corners.

Quilt Plan

FINISHING THE QUILT

Refer to "Finishing the Quilt" on page 22 to layer, baste, quilt, bind, and label your "Tessellating Blossoms" quilt.

QUILTING SUGGESTION

Stitching in the ditch is a good way to define the flower shapes, and it looks great. Just follow the lines that outline the blossoms. You might want to reinforce the suggestion of blossoms by embroidering a few French knots and stamens in the middle of some or all of the flowers. In the quilt shown, I quilted the flowers with black thread about ⅛" away from the ditch, just to add some definition to the motifs.

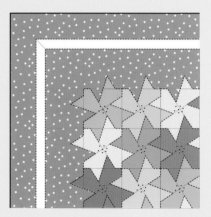

Here is another idea, a charming little curved-line quilting design to soften the angularity of the patchwork.

BONUS MINIATURE QUILT

The small spacer squares you set aside in step 4 are already pieced and ready to be made into a miniature version of the "Tessellating Pinwheels" quilt you made in steps 1–5. You cut it apart to make the "Tessellating Blossoms" blocks. Now you can make another one—in miniature!

1. Stitch the reserved blocks together into the pinwheel design. Press.

2. Cut two 1"-wide strips from the remaining white contrasting border fabric. Cut two 3"-wide strips from the remaining background/border (black polka-dot) print.

3. Stitch a narrow white strip to each of the background/border strips. Press. Use these to make mitered borders.

4. Finally, cut two strips, 2¼" x length of fabric. Use these to bind the quilt.

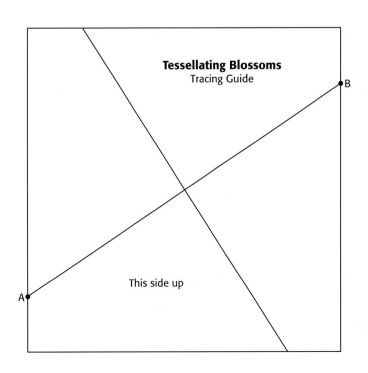

Tessellating Blossoms
Tracing Guide

B

This side up

A

Fractured Tessellations

Finished Size: 30" x 30"

This whimsical design was discovered quite by accident when a friend inadvertently flipped over her tracing guide. Instead of "Tessellating Blossoms" (page 35), she created a "Fractured Tessellations" quilt. To make this quilt, you start by making a "Tessellating Pinwheels" quilt like the one on page 31. Then cut it up and repiece it into an interestingly fractured design. It has a carefree look; don't try to match points.

MATERIALS

Yardages are based on 42"-wide fabric.

1¾ yards of light print for background, outer border, and binding

1¼ yards *total* of assorted dark and light prints (beiges, blacks, golds, greens, reds, tans) for pinwheels

¼ yard of black print for contrast border

1⅛ yards of backing fabric

34" x 34" piece of batting

Template plastic

Fine-point permanent marker (for template plastic)

Fine-point fabric marker

CUTTING

All strips are cut across the width of the fabric unless otherwise noted.

From the assorted prints, cut:

49 squares, 6" x 6"

From the light print, cut:

4 binding strips, 2½" x 42"

From the remaining light print, cut on the
lengthwise grain:

4 background strips, 3½" x length of fabric

4 background strips, 2¾" x length of fabric

4 border strips, 4" x length of fabric

From the black print, cut:

4 border strips, 2" x 42"

PIECING THE QUILT TOP

1. Arrange the 49 squares into a grid, 7 squares across and 7 squares down. Sew them together, referring to "Easy Chain Piecing" on page 17.

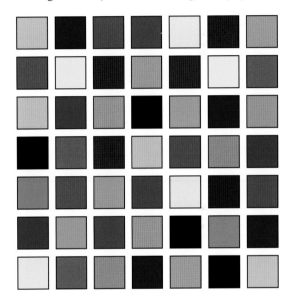

2. Stitch 3½"-wide light strips to the top and bottom edges of the patchwork. Trim to fit and press the seam allowances toward the edges. Stitch

3½"-wide light strips to the remaining sides of the patchwork. Trim to fit and press as before.

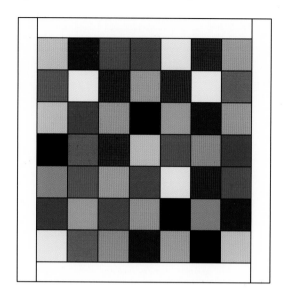

3. Make a plastic tracing guide by tracing all lines and notations from the pattern for "Tessellating Pinwheels" on page 34 onto template plastic. Make sure that the length of line AB is the same as the finished width of your blocks and adjust it, if necessary, before you cut out the guide.

4. Use the tracing guide to mark and cut 64 prepieced quadrille blocks. Keep them in order. Set aside the little spacer squares to use for another project.

5. Rotate and arrange the blocks into a new grid of 64 blocks, 8 across and 8 down. Chain piece the blocks together.

6. Sew 2¾"-wide light strips to the top and bottom of the patchwork grid. Trim to fit, and then press the seam allowances toward the outer edges. Sew 2¾"-wide light strips to the sides of the patchwork. Trim to fit and then press as before.

7. Make a smaller plastic tracing guide using the pattern for "Fractured Tessellations" on page 43.

Line AB on the tracing guide should measure exactly the same as the width across your finished Pinwheel blocks, from seam to seam. If it does not, make your tracing guide smaller or larger, adding or subtracting equal amounts on all sides.

8. Use the smaller tracing guide to mark and cut 81 prepieced quadrille blocks. Keep them in order.

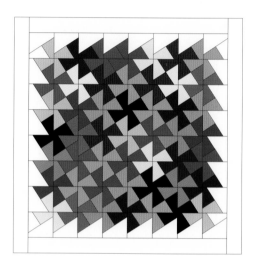

9. Rotate and arrange the blocks into a new grid of 81 blocks, 9 across and 9 down. Note that the blocks are rotated differently than in the practice place mat project on page 26. Chain piece the blocks together.

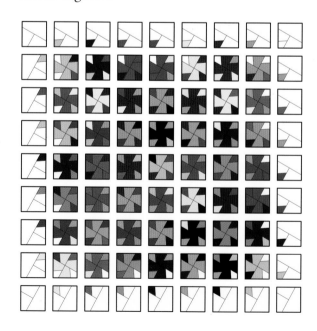

10. For a double final border, sew each of the 2"-wide black strips to a 4"-wide light strip. Referring to "Borders with Mitered Corners" on page 21, measure the quilt top, add the border strips with the black fabric adjoining the quilt top, and miter the corners.

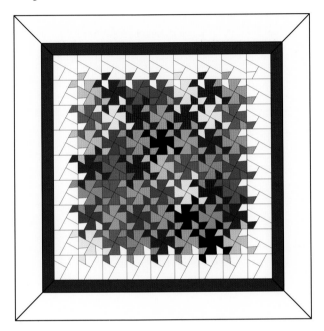

Quilt Plan

FINISHING THE QUILT

Refer to "Finishing the Quilt" on page 22 to layer, baste, quilt, bind, and label your "Fractured Tessellations" quilt.

QUILTING SUGGESTION

The quilt shown was machine quilted. I ignored the seams and quilted one free-form flower in the center of each pinwheel, using metallic thread to coordinate with the many metallic prints used in the quilt top. I quilted the inner border in the ditch and then stitched another row of straight line quilting through the center of the 4"-wide outer border.

Another similar quilt seemed to need a more carefree look, so I quilted a whole garden of fantasy flowers and spirals, and then filled in with many little four-petal blossoms. Curved lines fill the border area.

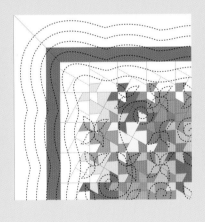

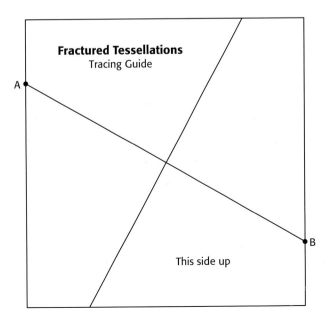

Fractured Tessellations
Tracing Guide

A

B

This side up

Flutterings I

Finished Size: 40" x 40"
Finished Block Size: 6½" x 6½"

The bright colors and fluttering action of butterfly wings inspired this unusual block. The BiRangle® tool came in handy to help give the simple pinwheel quilt an exciting new look. Where the blocks come together, you see smaller and a bit more subdued pinwheels I refer to as moths. The border magically becomes integrated into the design.

MATERIALS

Yardages are based on 42"-wide fabric.

1⅜ yards of light green for background

1¼ yards of medium green for border

⅜ yard of medium pink for butterflies

⅜ yard of medium purple for butterflies

¼ yard of dark pink for butterflies

¼ yard of pink check for moths

¼ yard of dark purple for butterflies

⅓ yard of purple solid for binding

1¼ yards of backing fabric

44" x 44" piece of batting

BiRangle ruler

Template plastic

Fine-point permanent marker (for template plastic)

Fine-point fabric marker

CUTTING

All strips are cut across the width of the fabric unless otherwise noted.

From the dark pink, cut:
13 squares, 4" x 4"

From the pink check, cut:
16 squares, 4" x 4"

From the dark purple, cut:
12 squares, 4" x 4"

From the light green, cut:
40 squares, 4" x 4"
2 strips, 12" x 42"

From the medium green, cut:
1 strip, 12" x 42"
4 background strips, 2½" x 42"
4 border strips, 4½" x 42"

From the medium pink, cut:
1 strip, 12" x 42"

From the medium purple, cut:
1 strip, 12" x 42"

From the purple solid, cut:
4 binding strips, 2½" x 42"

MAKING THE PATCHWORK GRID

1. Arrange the 13 dark pink, 16 pink check, 12 dark purple, and 40 light green squares into a grid of squares as shown below. Sew the squares together, referring to "Easy Chain Piecing" on page 17.

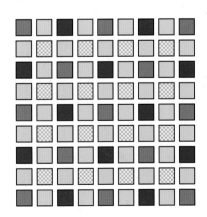

2. Stitch 2½"-wide medium green strips to the top and bottom edges of the patchwork. Trim to

fit. Press the seam allowances toward the outer edges. Stitch the remaining 2½"-wide medium green strips to the sides of the patchwork. Trim to fit. Press.

3. Make a plastic tracing guide by tracing all lines and notations from the pattern for "Flutterings I" on page 48 onto template plastic. Using the tracing guide, mark 100 prepieced quadrille blocks. *Do not cut them out yet.*

MAKING THE BIRANGLE UNITS

The BiRangle tool is so helpful when you want to make a batch of these versatile units. We'll be using it a little differently than the package directions, so set them aside until the next time you make a quilt with BiRangles. Follow these steps instead.

1. Layer all the 12" x 42" pieces of fabric right sides up (and in no particular order) on your cutting board.

2. Place the BiRangle *wrong* side up on the stack of fabrics, keeping the bottom ruler edge even with the bottom fabric edges. Place a long rotary-cutting ruler over both the fabric and BiRangle, lining up the ruler edge with the diagonal line on the BiRangle. Carefully remove the BiRangle without disturbing the long ruler. Cut through all five layers of fabric along the edge of the rotary-cutting ruler.

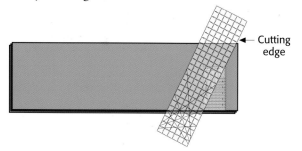

← Cutting edge

3. Make parallel cuts every 2¼" across the whole fabric surface. Recheck the angle frequently as you proceed to make sure you're still making accurate

cuts. Drop the four shortest stacks of strips into your scrap basket for use in a future project.

Set aside short strips of fabrics.

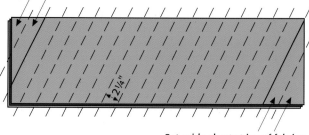

Set aside short strips of fabrics.

4. Arrange the full-sized strips into two strip sets. For the first strip set, alternate the medium pink strips and the light green strips for the first set until you've used all of the medium pink strips. Remove two of the light green strips from anywhere within the strip set and replace them with two medium green strips. Stitch the strips together with ¼"-wide seam allowances. Press the seam allowances open.

Replace 2 light green strips with medium green strips.

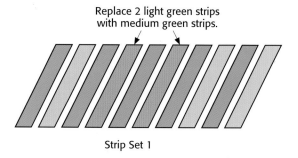

Strip Set 1

5. For the second strip set, alternate the medium purple strips and the light green strips, angled as shown. Remove one of the light green strips from anywhere within the set and replace it with a medium green strip. Stitch the strips together with ¼"-wide seam allowances. Press the seam allowances open.

Replace 1 light green strip with a medium green strip.

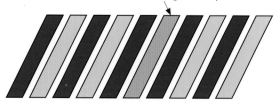

Strip Set 2

6. Place a strip set on your cutting board, right side up. Place the BiRangle face down near the top edge of the strip set and line up the diagonal line on the BiRangle with one of the seams. Place the rotary-cutting ruler's edge against the top edge of the BiRangle. Remove the BiRangle and trim the top edge of the strip sets.

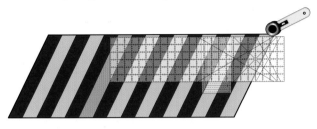

7. Cut four 3"-wide strips parallel to the first cut.

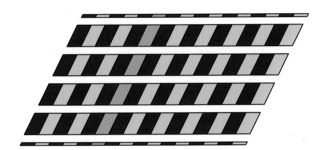

8. Working with one of the pieced strips at a time, start at the right end (reverse if you are left-handed) and place the BiRangle face down over the first diagonal seam, with the top edge of the tool over the cut edge at the top of the pieced strip. Cut along the right edge of the BiRangle. Move left to the next seam. Repeat across the width of the strip.

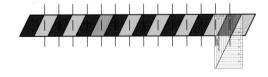

9. Continue cutting BiRangle units from both of the original strip sets until you have the following units.

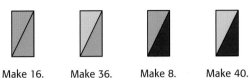

Make 16.   Make 36.   Make 8.   Make 40.

PIECING THE QUILT TOP

You now have everything you need to piece 25 intricate-looking blocks. They are actually simple nine patches!

1. Beginning in one corner of the patchwork grid, cut four blocks at a time from your pieced grid of 100 quadrille blocks. Combine them with the appropriate BiRangle units and the reserved spacer squares to make one 6½" block at a time. You will need the following color combinations to complete your quilt top.

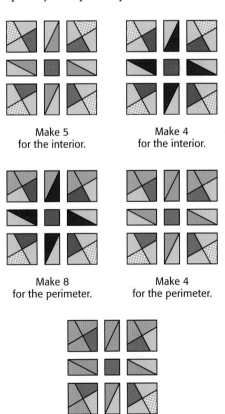

Make 5
for the interior.

Make 4
for the interior.

Make 8
for the perimeter.

Make 4
for the perimeter.

Make 4
for the corners.

CHECKPOINT

The BiRangle units that include the border fabric go only on the outside edges of the perimeter blocks.

2. Arrange the 25 blocks into a grid of 5 across and 5 down. Be sure that the border fabric only appears around the perimeter as shown in the quilt plan below. Also, in the quilt shown, the pink and purple blocks are alternated, and the pink blocks are in the corners of the quilt.

3. Use your favorite speed-piecing method to stitch the blocks together. Press.

4. Use the 4½"-wide medium green strips for the final border. Referring to "Borders with Butted Corners" on page 20, measure the quilt top and add border strips to the top and bottom and then to the sides. Press the seam allowances toward the borders.

Quilt Plan

FINISHING THE QUILT

Refer to "Finishing the Quilt" on page 22 to layer, baste, quilt, bind, and label your "Flutterings I" quilt.

QUILTING SUGGESTION

The quilt shown was machine quilted in an allover meandering pattern. Other ideas would be to quilt in the ditch around the fluttering shapes in these blocks or quilt a curved design as shown.

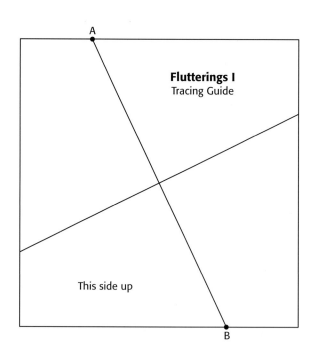

A

Flutterings I
Tracing Guide

This side up

B

Flutterings II

Finished Size: 57" x 76½"
Finished Block Size: 6½" x 6½"

Three background fabrics in light, medium, and dark values frame the action, anchoring a floating array of spinning stars. Small pinwheels seem to fade in and out, sometimes blending with the background and sometimes taking their places among the bright stars. Lovers of patchwork will enjoy assembling this puzzle, but it's not for the faint of heart! I recommend that you choose your fabrics in the order they're given in the materials list for best results. Be sure to enter this one in the next quilt show. It's a crowd pleaser!

MATERIALS

Yardages are based on 42"-wide fabric.

2⅝ yards of large-scale black print for background, outer border, and binding

2 yards of gold print for background

1 yard of light print for background

¼ yard of dark olive print for pinwheels

⅜ yard of medium olive print for pinwheels

½ yard of light olive for pinwheels

½ yard *each* of 5 red prints for stars

½ yard *each* of 5 black-and-gold prints for stars

5 yards of backing fabric

61" x 81" piece of batting

BiRangle ruler

Template plastic

Fine-point permanent marker (for template plastic)

Fine-point fabric marker

CUTTING

All strips are cut across the width of the fabric unless otherwise noted.

From the large-scale black print, cut on the lengthwise grain:

 3 border strips, 6" x 80"; crosscut 1 of the strips into 4 pieces, 17½" long

 4 strips, 2½" x 70½"; from 2 of the strips, cut 4 pieces, 14½" long, and 2 pieces, 18" long

From the remaining large-scale black print, cut:

 36 squares, 4" x 4"

 2 rectangles, 18" x 42"

 2 border strips, 4" x 12¼"

 7 binding strips, 2½" x 42"

From the gold print, cut:

 64 squares, 4" x 4"

 2 rectangles, 18" x 42"

From the light print, cut:

 29 strips, 4" x 4"

 1 rectangle, 18" x 42"

From the dark olive print, cut:

 10 squares, 4" x 4"

From the medium olive print, cut:

 18 squares, 4" x 4"

From the light olive print, cut:

 30 squares, 4" x 4"

Layer all of the assorted red prints right side up and cut:

 7 diagonal strips, 2¼" wide*

From *each* of the five red prints, also cut:

 7 squares, 4" x 4" (35 total)

 7 squares, 1¾" x 1¾" (35 total)

Layer all of the assorted black-and-gold prints right side up and cut:

 7 diagonal strips, 2¼" wide*

From *each* of the five black-and-gold prints, also cut:

 7 squares, 4" x 4" (35 total)

 7 squares, 1¾" x 1¾" (35 total)

*Use the BiRangle tool to determine the correct angle and direction of cut for these strips, referring to the directions on page 46.

MAKING THE PATCHWORK GRID

1. Arrange all of the 4" x 4" squares as shown below into a grid of squares. Chain sew the squares together except for the shorter top and bottom rows. Press.

2. Place the shorter 2½"-wide black strips next to the squares of the top and bottom rows as shown. Stitch together the top and bottom rows; add them to the grid of squares. Press. Trim the long 2½"-wide black strips to fit the two side edges of the grid. Stitch the strips in place. Press.

2½" x 18"

2½" x 14½"   2½" x 14½"

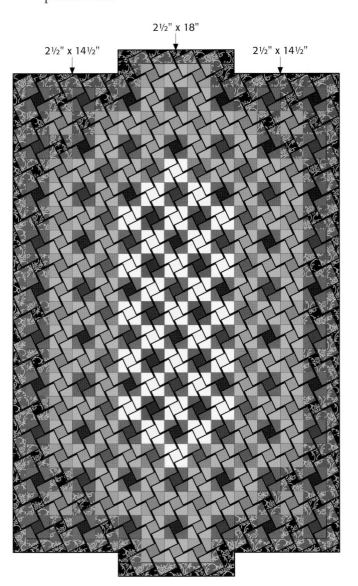

3. Make a tracing guide by tracing all lines and notations from the "Flutterings I" guide on page 48 onto template plastic. Use the tracing guide to mark quadrille blocks over the whole surface of your patchwork. Because there are so many quadrille blocks in assorted color combinations, try cutting out only one third of the blocks at a time, working from the top down. Place the cut blocks in order on the floor or on a design wall, spacing them in groups of four so that they form pinwheels, and leaving space between the four-unit groupings to allow room for the BiRangle units (star points) we'll make in steps 4 and 5. Place a matching 1¾" square in the center of each pinwheel formed by the quadrilles.

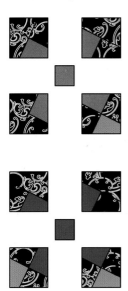

MAKING THE BIRANGLE UNITS

1. Layer the 18" x 42" rectangles of black print, gold print, and light print right sides up on your cutting mat.

2. Referring to steps 2 and 3 of "Making the BiRangle Units" on page 46, cut the black, gold, and light background fabrics into 2¼"-wide diagonal strips. *Do not sew the strips together.*

3. Examine the quilt layout one pinwheel at a time to determine what colors you need to sew together to make the BiRangle star points. If the pinwheel arms are black, the block needs a red fabric for the long star points, so choose one of the red diagonal strips. (Conversely, if the pinwheel arms are red, then you'll need black star points.) Next, decide which of the three background-fabric strips to stitch next to the red strip: the large-scale black print, the gold print, or the light print. The adjacent fabric patches in the pinwheel pieces will always indicate the correct choice.

4. Stitch the red strip to the appropriate background strip. Left to right or right to left, it doesn't matter! Gently press the seam open. Then use the BiRangle tool to cut four perfect BiRangle units, each 3⅛" x 1¾". You may need all four identical units for your first star, or you may need only one, two, or three for now. Set the unused units aside; they will surely be needed for another star.

Combine another strip of this same red fabric with a different background strip and cut BiRangle units as needed to complete this star. Set the four new BiRangle units into the design, but do not sew yet.

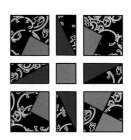 

5. Continue to make star points, one at a time, adding red star points to black pinwheels and black star points to red pinwheels. Each star point is a

BiRangle unit with the background color chosen to go with the adjacent patchwork. Set aside the extra BiRangle units; check your growing collection of extras often to see if they can be used in the next star. You'll eventually need them, and it all comes out about right in the end. You may have some leftovers, but not too many.

6. After making and placing all of the pieces for a large section of your quilt, stand back and study it to see that everything is in order. Each star should have four pinwheel arms, four long points, and a center square that matches the pinwheel arms. Backgrounds should flow uninterrupted within each block. Once you are satisfied that all pieces are in their correct places, you can sew the units together into rows. And sew the rows together quickly before a breeze disturbs your arrangement! Press well.

7. Continue on to the next large section of units. When you've gotten each large portion of the quilt assembled, sew the sections together to complete the interior of the quilt top.

8. Measure the quilt top through the vertical center. Trim the two longest 6"-wide border strips to this length and sew them to the sides of the quilt top. Press the seam allowances toward the borders. In the same manner, measure the width of the quilt top, trim the remaining border strips to this length, and sew them to the top and bottom of the quilt top. Press as before.

FINISHING THE QUILT

Refer to "Finishing the Quilt" on page 22 to layer, baste, quilt, bind, and label your "Flutterings II" quilt.

Quilt Plan

QUILTING SUGGESTION

The quilt shown was machine quilted. I chose a spinning design that fits into the shapes and adds to the excited movement of the patchwork stars. In the border, I meander quilted, making large jigsaw-puzzle shapes. Some straight-line quilting might look great too.

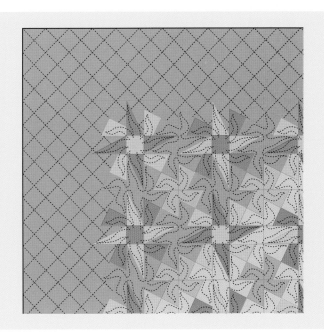

Kissing Links

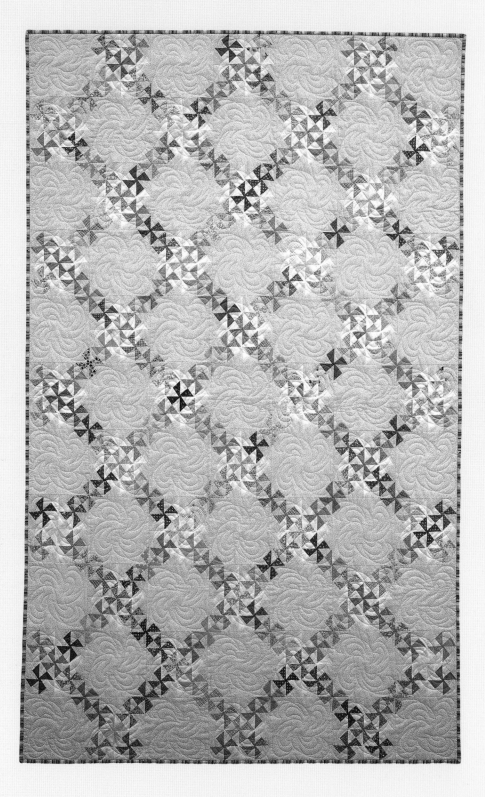

Finished Size: 61" x 96"

Chains of tiny pinwheels dance across this quilt with all the charm of a traditional Irish Chain design, but with a joie de vivre that knows no boundaries. The individual blocks are speed-pieced and then joined by the kiss of an extra pinwheel. The best scrap quilts are made with many more fabrics than 10, so I encourage you to use as many pastels as you can find.

MATERIALS

Yardages are based on 42"-wide fabric.

1⅞ yards of white fabric

⅜ yards *each* of 10 assorted pastel prints

6½ yards of yellow print for background

⅝ yard of multicolored stripe for binding

5¾ yards of backing fabric

65" x 100" piece of batting

Template plastic

Fine-point permanent marker (for template plastic)

Fine-point fabric marker

CUTTING

All strips are cut across the width of the fabric unless otherwise noted.

From *each* pastel print, cut:

 3 strips, 4" x 42"; set aside 1 strip of each fabric; then from the remaining strips, cut 190 squares, 4" x 4"

From the white fabric, cut:

 16 strips, 4" x 42"; crosscut into 152 squares, 4" x 4"

From the yellow print, cut:

 5 strips, 11" x 42"; crosscut into 76 pieces, 2¼" x 11"

 5 strips, 15" x 42"; crosscut into 76 pieces, 2¼" x 15"

 10 strips, 9¼" x 42"; crosscut into 39 squares, 9¼" x 9¼"*

From the multicolored stripe, cut:

 8 binding strips, 2½" x 42"

*Cut the yellow 9¼" squares only after you have completed at least one of the pieced blocks. They must be cut the same size, so adjust the size of the yellow squares if necessary.

MAKING THE PIECED BLOCKS

Make the pieced blocks one at a time until you get the hang of it. Then you may enjoy working on four at a time—a good hour's work.

1. For each block, choose five different pastel squares and four white squares. Arrange them in a nine-patch formation, three across and three down, alternating colored and white squares. Stitch the squares together into a Nine Patch block, referring to "Easy Chain Piecing" on page 17. You'll need a total of 38 blocks for the quilt.

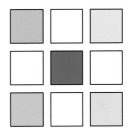

2. Sew the 2¼" x 11" yellow strips to the top and bottom of the Nine Patch blocks, trim to fit, and then press the seam allowances toward the outer edge. Add the 2¼" x 15" yellow strips to the sides of the blocks in the same manner.

3. Make a plastic tracing guide, using the "Kissing Links" tracing guide pattern on page 58.

4. Use the tracing guide to mark and cut out 16 prepieced quadrille blocks from each Nine Patch block.

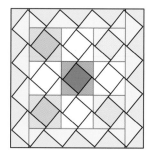

5. Arrange them in order in a grid of 16 blocks, 4 across and 4 down. Chain piece the grid together.

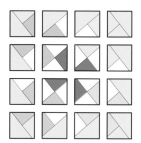

6. Repeat steps 1–5 until you have completed all 38 pieced blocks. Measure the pieced blocks from cut edge to cut edge. Use this measurement to cut the 39 yellow squares.

7. Arrange the 38 pieced blocks with the 39 plain blocks, alternating them in a grid of 7 blocks

across and 11 blocks down. Place a plain block at each of the corners. *Don't sew them together yet.*

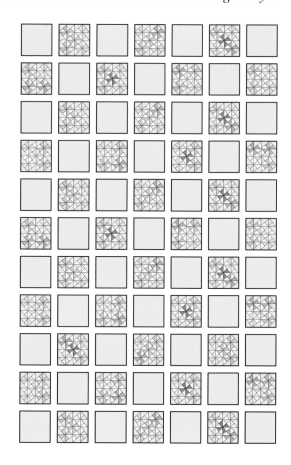

MAKING THE KISSING LINKS

The pinwheels that connect the blocks and complete the illusion of intersecting diagonal chains are each made up of four links. At each point where four blocks meet, you will need four identical kissing links, one for the corner of each block. Exception: No links are needed around the outside edges of the quilt.

1. Use the 4" x 42" pastel strips that you set aside earlier. Stack as many strips, all right side up, as you can accurately cut with your best pair of scissors (between four and eight layers).

2. Make a plastic template, using the "Kissing Links" appliqué pattern on page 58.

3. Place the template on top of the stack of strips. Position it with the grain-line arrow on either the lengthwise or the crosswise grain of the fabric strips and trace around it. Reposition the template and trace around it again, continuing along the strips. Cut through all layers at once on your drawn lines to release little stacks of kissing links. You will need four matching links for each block intersection.

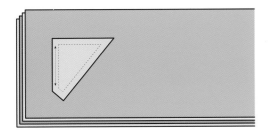

4. At each block intersection, pin four matching links in place, one on each of the four blocks.

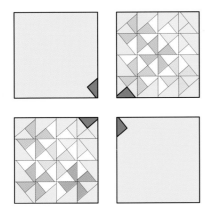

5. Fold under and press the two outer straight-grain edges, and then appliqué each link into place. I like to do this by machine, but it also makes for very pleasant handwork. Leave the bias edges unsewn.

SHORTCUT
MACHINE APPLIQUÉ

Thread your machine with clear monofilament thread in the top and regular sewing thread in the bobbin. Use a Sharp #11 needle. Loosen the top tension to nearly 0 to accommodate the thin nylon thread. Set the stitch length to a long stitch (3.5 or 4). Set the stitch width to the narrowest zigzag. Stitch along the folded edge of the "Kissing Links" appliqué piece, with the needle stepping on and off the edge.

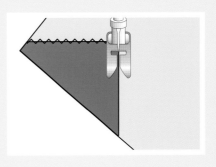

ASSEMBLING THE QUILT TOP

1. Stitch together the 77-block grid, referring to "Easy Chain Piecing." Sew the blocks together in rows, and then sew the rows together. Take care to keep the blocks in order so that the "Kissing Links" appliqués will all be the same color where four blocks come together.

2. Press carefully with steam one last time. This quilt doesn't have a border attached, so you will have a lot of seams along the edges. Be careful to not stretch them out of shape as you press. Also note that if you used nylon monofilament thread for your appliqué stitches, you should use a

pressing cloth for this final pressing. This thread has been known to melt and disappear, one of my worst nightmares.

FINISHING THE QUILT

Refer to "Finishing the Quilt" on page 22 to layer, baste, quilt, bind, and label your "Kissing Links" quilt.

QUILTING SUGGESTION

Check your favorite quilt shop for a quilting stencil or continuous-line quilting design to use in the centers of the plain blocks. This wide-open space is perfect for showcasing your hand or machine quilting!

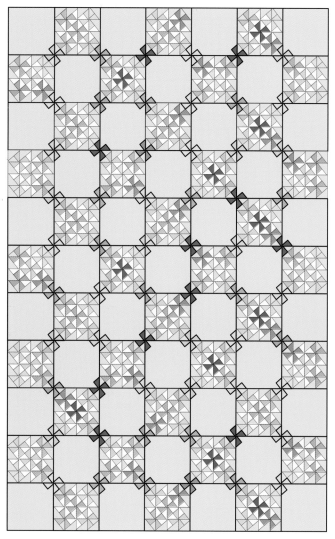

Quilt Plan

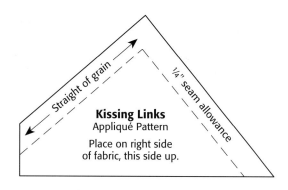

Straight of grain

¼" seam allowance

Kissing Links
Appliqué Pattern

Place on right side
of fabric, this side up.

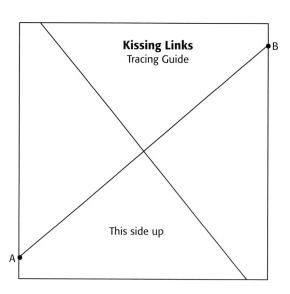

Kissing Links
Tracing Guide

B

A

This side up

Hand in Hand
Wall Hanging

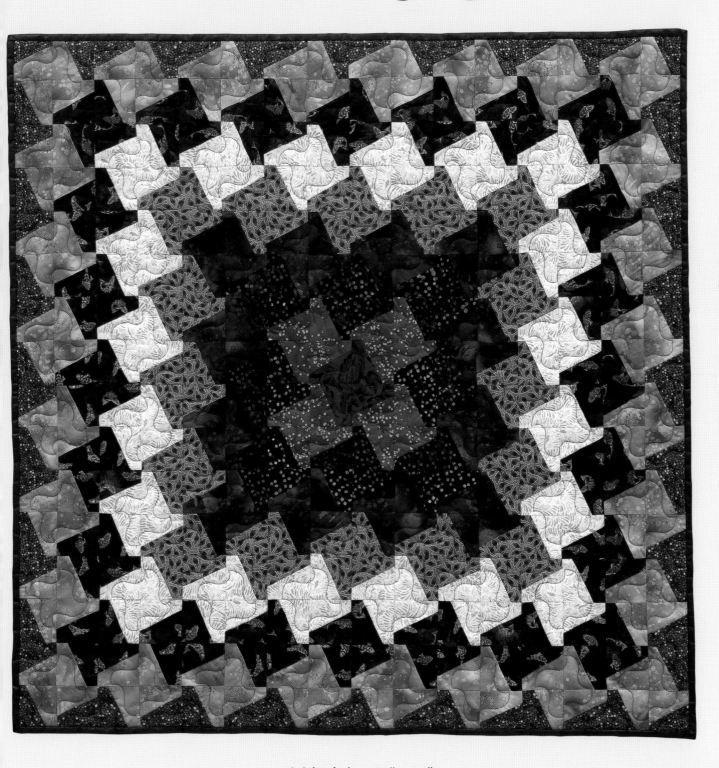

Finished size: 54" x 54"

Even if you don't make this easy little piece, take a few minutes to read through the following instructions before starting the bed-sized houndstooth quilts. With a few changes, the larger quilt is made using the same method. In this version, nine coordinating fabrics in shades of blue, teal, and purple go around and around, building a simple shape into a complex pattern.

MATERIALS

Yardages are based on 42"-wide fabric.

⅛ yard of fabric A

¼ yard of fabric B

¼ yard of fabric C

⅜ yard of fabric D

⅜ yard of fabric E

½ yard of fabric F

⅝ yard of fabric G

⅔ yard of fabric H

⅔ yard of fabric I

½ yard of binding fabric

2½ yards of backing fabric

58" x 58" piece of batting

Template plastic

Fine-point permanent marker (for template plastic)

Fine-point fabric marker

CUTTING

All strips are cut across the width of the fabric unless otherwise noted.

From fabric A, cut:

  1 strip, 3½" x 42"

From fabric B, cut:

  2 strips, 3½" x 42"

From fabric C, cut:

  2 strips, 3½" x 42"

From fabric D, cut:

  3 strips, 3½" x 42"

From fabric E, cut:

  3 strips, 3½" x 42"

From fabric F, cut:

  4 strips, 3½" x 42"

From fabric G, cut:

  5 strips, 3½" x 42"

From fabric H, cut:

  6 strips, 3½" x 42"

From fabric I, cut:

  6 strips, 3½" x 42"

From the binding fabric, cut:

  5 strips, 2½" x 42"

PIECING THE BLOCKS

1. Sew the two fabric B strips together end to end. Repeat with the two fabric C strips. Continue in the same manner, sewing the strips of the same fabric together end to end.

2. Sew the strips together lengthwise in order from fabric A through I to make a graduated strip set as shown below. Use a scant ¼"-wide seam allowance. Press all seam allowances in the same direction, either toward the top or the bottom of the strip set.

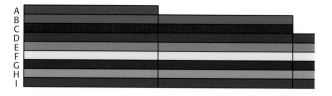

3. Make a plastic tracing guide, using the pattern for "Hand in Hand Wall Hanging" on page 63. This tracing guide helps you cut an interesting and very useful little block. I call it a twin square because it has two identical parts.

4. Position the tracing guide at the widest short end of the strip set so that the diagonal line on the guide is aligned with one of the seams in the strip set. Trace around the guide and set it aside.

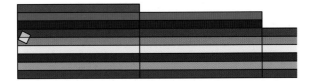

5. Place the widest end of the strip set on your cutting mat. Turn it so the strip set is positioned vertically to make cutting easier. Place a long rotary-cutting ruler along the edge of the traced twin square, taking care to align the edge of the ruler exactly with the marked line of the twin square as shown. Use a rotary cutter to make a cut from one side of the strip set to the other.

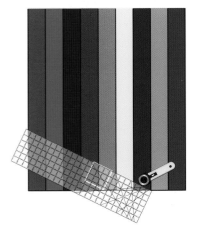

6. Cut strips parallel to the first cut and 3⅛" apart (the width of the tracing guide). Use the tracing guide often to check the angle of your cuts. If necessary, reposition the guide and cut an accurate edge from time to time.

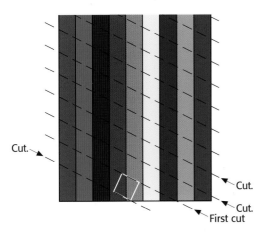

7. Place the tracing guide over a seam on one of the strips and trace against the left and right sides to mark a twin square. Move the guide to the next seam and continue marking squares, one at a time, along the length of the strip.

8. Cut on the marked lines with a rotary cutter or scissors. Stack identical twin squares together. Discard any twin squares that have unintentional seams running across them, where the strips were joined end to end; you won't need them.

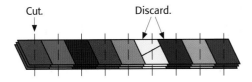

PIECING THE QUILT TOP

1. Begin with the smallest stack of twin squares, which are composed of fabrics A and B. Place four squares together as shown, so that fabric A makes the shape of a houndstooth check and fabric B is around the perimeter.

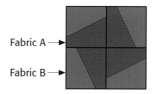

2. Using the next smallest stack of twin squares, which is composed of fabrics B and C, place 12 of these around the first four blocks. Turn them so that four complete houndstooth-check shapes of fabric B surround the center houndstooth. Fabric C is now around the perimeter.

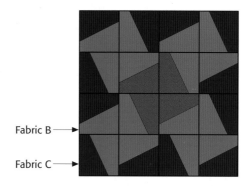

3. Place the 20 blocks in the next smallest stack around the outside and complete the third round of houndstooth checks in fabric C. Continue adding rounds in this way until all of the stacks are used up and your work surface is covered by a grid of 256 twin squares, 16 across and 16 down. Step back and study the grid carefully from a distance to make sure that all squares are positioned correctly.

4. Use your favorite fast-piecing method or refer to "Easy Chain Piecing" on page 17 to stitch the grid together. Press well.

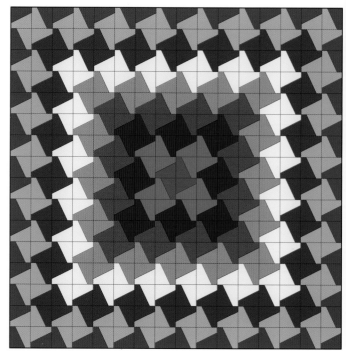

Quilt Plan

FINISHING THE QUILT

Refer to "Finishing the Quilt" on page 22 to layer, baste, quilt, bind, and label your "Hand in Hand Wall Hanging." Note that the quilt does not have an outer border, so it's a good idea to machine stitch around the perimeter of the quilt top before layering, basting, and quilting your project. Stitch between ⅛" and ¼" from the edges to stabilize the bias-cut pieces and prevent them from stretching.

Hand in Hand Wall Hanging

QUILTING SUGGESTION

These shapes look good with traditional outline quilting, ¼" away from the seams. The seams within the houndstooth shapes, however, should not be emphasized. Rather, fill in the center areas with a simple figure. In the quilt shown, a shape similar to the houndstooth pattern was used, but it has rounded rather than squared-off legs. Here is another easy quilting design to use.

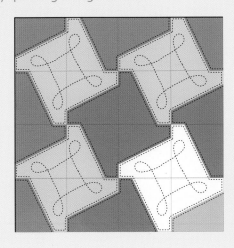

BONUS PROJECT

This bright and cheerful baby quilt is made in the same manner as "Hand in Hand Wall Hanging." The strips are cut the same width and the twin square blocks are cut in the same fashion. But rather than have a grid of 256 squares, this quilt uses seven rather than nine fabrics, so the grid is 144 squares, laid out 12 blocks by 12 blocks.

To make the quilt finish the same size as the main project, a border of fabric G has been added. To do this, you'll need one yard extra of fabric G to cut five border strips, 6" x 42". Referring to "Borders with Butted Corners" on page 20, measure the quilt top, trim the borders to fit, and attach them to the quilt top. For the top and bottom borders, you'll need to sew three of the border strips together end to end, and from the long strip, cut two borders to fit your quilt top.

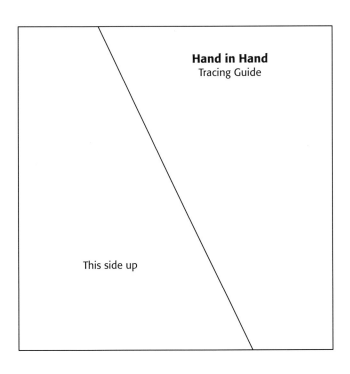

Hand in Hand
Tracing Guide

This side up

Hand in Hand
around the Commons

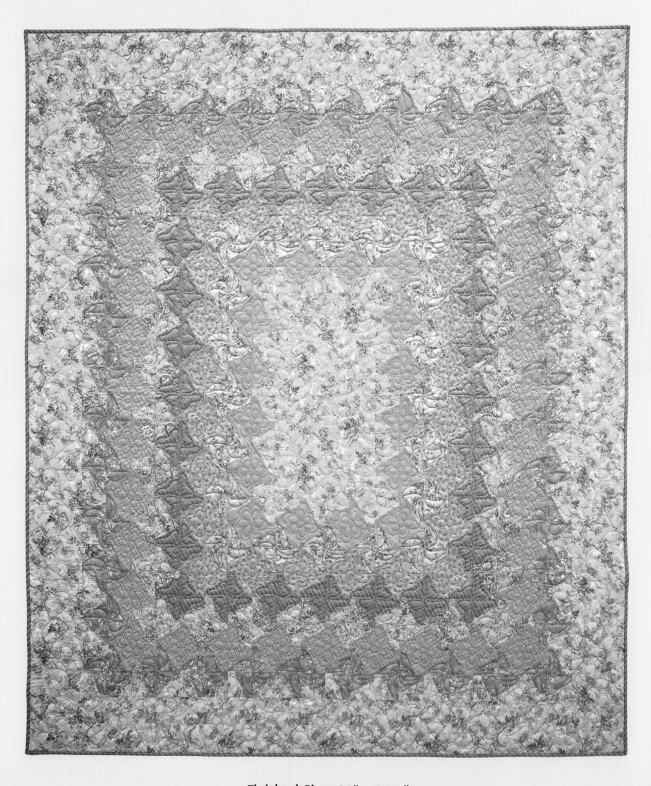

Finished Size: 81" x 94½"

This quilt resembles the traditional "Boston Commons" patchwork pattern, but with a new twist. Choose a main fabric and seven fabrics that coordinate with it. For my version, I chose a large-scale yellow floral print for the main fabric. Determine the order in which the seven coordinating fabrics will appear in your quilt before purchasing them, because the yardage required for each fabric depends on that order.

MATERIALS

Yardages are based on 42"-wide fabric.

4⅜ yards of main print for center panel, patchwork, and borders

½ yard of fabric A

⅝ yard of fabric B

¾ yard of fabric C

⅞ yard of fabric D

1 yard of fabric E

1⅛ yards of fabric F

1¼ yards of fabric G

1 yard of striped fabric for bias binding, *or* ¾ yard of other fabric for straight-grain binding

5½ yards of backing fabric

85" x 100" piece of batting

Template plastic

Fine-point permanent marker (for template plastic)

Fine-point fabric marker

CUTTING

All strips are cut across the width of the fabric unless otherwise noted.

From fabric A, cut:

4 strips, 4" x 42"

From fabric B, cut:

5 strips, 4" x 42"

From fabric C, cut:

6 strips, 4" x 42"

From fabric D, cut:

7 strips, 4" x 42"

From fabric E, cut:

8 strips, 4" x 42"

From fabric F, cut:

9 strips, 4" x 42"

From fabric G, cut:

10 strips, 4" x 42"

From the main print, cut on the *lengthwise* grain:

2 border strips, 8" x 96"

2 border strips, 8" x 68½"

From the remaining main print, cut:

1 center panel, 14¼" x 28"

14 strips, 4" x 42"

From the striped binding fabric, cut:

Enough 2½"-wide bias strips to yield 360" of binding, *or*

9 strips, 2½" x 42", for straight-grain binding

PIECING THE BLOCKS

1. Sew same-fabric strips together end to end to make long strips of each of fabrics A–G. With the main print make two long pieces, one composed of four 42"-long strips and the other composed of ten 42"-long strips.

2. Make a graduated strip set by stitching the long strips together lengthwise. Begin with the strip made of four main-print strips, next use the fabric A strip, and continue in alphabetical order. End with the strip made of 10 main-print segments. Press all seam allowances in the same direction.

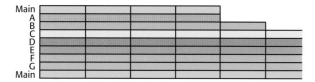

3. Make a tracing guide, using the pattern for "Hand in Hand around the Commons" on page 68. Position the tracing guide at the widest short end of the strip set so that the diagonal line on the guide is aligned with one of the seams in the strip set. Trace around the guide and set it aside.

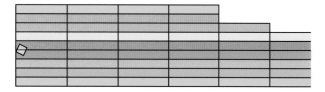

4. Place the widest end of the strip set on your cutting mat. Turn it so the strip set is positioned vertically to make cutting easier. Place a long rotary-cutting ruler along the edge of the traced twin square, taking care to align the edge of the ruler exactly with the marked line of the twin square as shown. Use a rotary cutter to make a cut from one side of the strip set to the other.

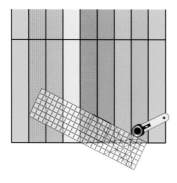

5. Cut strips parallel to the first cut and 3⅞" apart (the width of your guide). Place the tracing guide over a seam and check the angle before each cut. (If the cut edge is not even with the edge of the guide, make a fresh cut at the correct angle before cutting the next strip.) Continue cutting 3⅞"-wide strips along the entire length of the strip set until you have 26 segments.

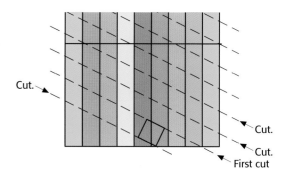

6. Place the tracing guide over a seam and trace against the left and right sides to mark a twin square. Move the guide to the next seam and continue marking squares, one at a time, down the length of the strip.

7. Cut on the marked lines with a rotary cutter or scissors. Stack identical twin squares together. Discard the twin squares that have unintentional seams running across them, where the strips were joined end to end; you won't need them.

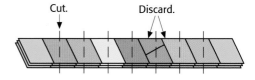

ASSEMBLING THE QUILT TOP

1. Place the 14¼" x 28" main-print center panel in the center of your table or design wall. Using the smallest stack of twin squares, which are composed of the main print and fabric A, surround the center rectangle with twin squares as shown.

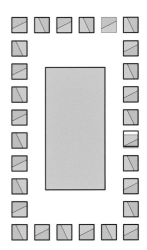

2. Using the next smallest stack of twin squares, which are composed of fabrics A and B, add another round of squares.

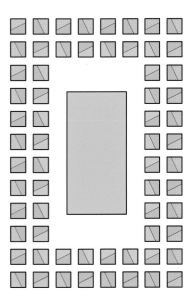

3. Continue placing twin squares in the same manner until eight rounds of squares surround the center panel.

4. To speed-piece the blocks together, it's easiest to work in sections because there will be less chance of getting a twin square in the wrong position. First, arrange and sew together the blocks above the center rectangle. Next, sew together the blocks below the rectangle. Sew together the blocks to the left and right of the rectangle, and finally the blocks in the corners, referring to the assembly diagram below.

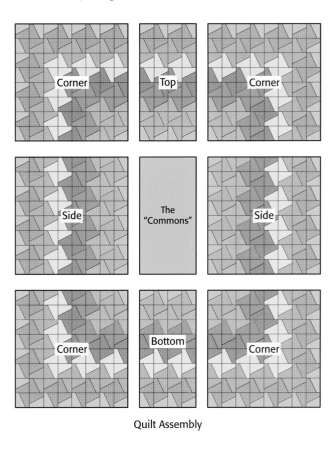

Quilt Assembly

5. Sew the side sections to the center rectangle.

6. Sew the top and bottom sections to the corner sections; then sew them to the center section. Press.

7. Referring to "Borders with Butted Corners" on page 20, measure the quilt top and add the 8"-wide border.

Quilt Plan

FINISHING THE QUILT

Refer to "Finishing the Quilt" on page 22 to layer, baste, quilt, bind, and label your "Hand in Hand around the Commons" quilt.

QUILTING SUGGESTION

I sent my quilt top off to a good machine quilter, who set off the patchwork design by quilting whimsical flowers and curved pinwheels in alternating rounds of the quilt. Beautiful feathers quilted in the border frame the quilt.

**Hand in Hand
around the Commons**
Tracing Guide

This side up

Mountain Trails

Finished Size: 57" x 72"

Set in its most basic arrangement, the Rocky Mountain Sparkler blocks march across the quilt top in rows. For the mountains and background, I used mostly solids or small-scale prints so that the multiple seams in each block are not so noticeable. I reserved the use of a large-scale print for the double outer border.

MATERIALS

Yardages are based on 42"-wide fabric.

2¾ yards of black floral print for inner and outer borders and binding

2 yards of tan check for background

1¼ yards *total* of assorted solids or muted prints in rose, blue, green, and black (5 fat quarters would work well)

⅜ yard of light blue solid for middle border

3 yards of backing fabric

61" x 76" piece of batting

CUTTING

All strips are cut across the width of the fabric unless otherwise noted.

From the assorted solids or muted prints, cut:

21 squares, 8½" x 8½"

From the tan check, cut:

21 squares, 8½" x 8½"

From the light blue solid, cut:

7 border strips, 2¼" x 42"

From the black floral print, cut:

7 binding strips, 2½" x 42"

From the remaining black floral print, cut on the *lengthwise* **grain:**

8 border strips, 4½" x length of fabric

MAKING THE BLOCKS

1. Pair the assorted solid or print 8½" squares with the 8½" tan check squares and make Twin Triangle blocks, referring to page 14. Cut each pair of Twin Triangles into four strips, each 2" wide.

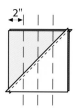

2. Arrange the block segments as shown below, and then sew them together to make 21 Rocky Mountain Sparkler blocks.

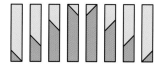

Make 21.

ASSEMBLING THE QUILT TOP

1. Arrange the blocks into seven horizontal rows of three blocks each. When you are pleased with your color arrangement, sew the blocks together into rows. Press the vertical seams in opposite directions from row to row.

2. Stitch the rows together and press all seam allowances in one direction.

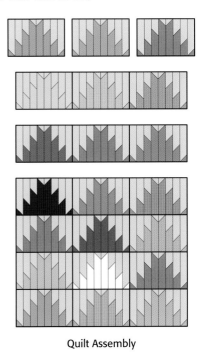

Quilt Assembly

3. Sew the 2¼"-wide blue strips together end to end into one long strip. From this strip, cut two strips 70" long and two strips 50" long.

4. Referring to "Borders with Mitered Corners" on page 21, make a multistrip unit for each side of the quilt top. Sew a 4½"-wide black floral strip to either side of the four blue strips. Press the seam allowances toward the black fabric.

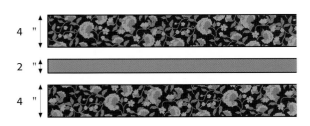

4"

2"

4"

5. Sew the strips to the edges of the quilt top and miter the corners, carefully matching each strip.

Quilt Plan

FINISHING THE QUILT

Refer to "Finishing the Quilt" on page 22 to layer, baste, quilt, bind, and label your "Mountain Trails" quilt.

 QUILTING SUGGESTION

To make this a quick-and-easy comforter project, I used a fat batt and simple quilting in horizontal rows of undulating waves to mimic mountain shapes. Left unadorned, these simple mountain shapes have a quiet dignity. However, they also provide an ideal surface for decoration. You might want to try some fancy machine-embroidery stitches to create meandering trails across the slopes, and then quilt in the ditch along the jagged mountaintops.

Tribble Trouble

Finished size: 60" x 75"

The trouble with Tribbles, as all Star Trek fans know, is that these cute, fuzzy little creatures multiply rapidly and cannot be confined. In this quilt, the blocks—like Tribbles—tumble right over the borders in search of mischief. The blocks are easy and quick to make. Try using them in Log Cabin–style block settings.

MATERIALS

Yardages are based on 42"-wide fabric.

1⅞ yards of large-scale floral batik for outer border

1¾ yards *total* (7 fat quarters) of assorted solids for blocks: peach, orange, red, light green, gold, burgundy, taupe

1½ yards of dark batik for background

¾ yard of striped fabric for blocks

⅝ yard of small-scale dark batik for inner border

⅝ yard of black solid for binding

3¾ yards of backing fabric

66" x 81" piece of batting

CUTTING

All strips are cut across the width of the fabric unless otherwise noted.

From the dark batik background fabric, cut:

24 squares, 8½" x 8½"

From the assorted solids, cut:

28 squares, 8½" x 8½"

From the striped fabric, cut:

56 rectangles, 2" x 8"

From the large-scale floral batik, cut on the *lengthwise* grain:

2 strips, 6½" x 52"

From the remaining large-scale floral batik, cut:

4 strips, 6½" x 20"

2 strips, 6½" x 30"

4 squares, 8½" x 8½"

From the small-scale dark batik, cut:

2 strips, 2" x 42"

From the black solid, cut:

7 binding strips, 2½" x 42"

MAKING THE BLOCKS

For this quilt, make Rocky Mountain Sparkler blocks (page 14) but with some important differences.

1. Pair each of the 8½" dark batik squares with an 8½" solid square to make Twin Triangle units.

2. Stack the units right side up and oriented the same way (dark side over dark side). Cut the half-square triangle units into four strips, each 2" wide.

 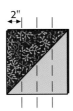

Stack right side up.

3. Rearrange the strips, mixing colors randomly, and sew them together into Rocky Mountain Sparkler half blocks. Add a 2" x 8" striped rectangle to the left edge of each unit, as shown, to make the Tribble blocks.

Make 48
Tribble blocks.

4. Arrange all the Tribble blocks into groups of four and sew them together as shown.

Make 12.

5. Pair the remaining four 8½" solid squares with the 8½" floral batik squares. Follow steps 1–3 to make eight Breakout blocks for the borders.

Make 8
Breakout blocks.

ASSEMBLING THE QUILT TOP

1. Arrange the Tribble blocks in four horizontal rows of three blocks each.

2. Sew the blocks together into rows, pressing the seams in opposite directions from row to row. Then sew the rows together, matching the seams at the block intersections. Steam press.

3. Sew the eight Breakout blocks together into pairs as shown.

Make 4.

4. Using the pairs of Breakout blocks and the inner- and outer-border strips, assemble the pieced borders as shown.

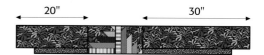

Top and Bottom Borders

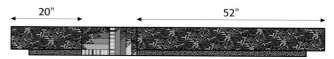

Side Borders

5. Referring to the quilt plan below, sew the borders to the quilt top, taking care to match the seams of the border blocks with the seams of the blocks. Begin and end the stitching ¼" from the corners of the quilt top.

6. Referring to "Borders with Mitered Corners" on page 21, miter the corners. Press.

Quilt Plan

FINISHING THE QUILT

Refer to "Finishing the Quilt" on page 22 to layer, baste, quilt, bind, and label your "Tribble Trouble" quilt.

QUILTING SUGGESTION

The groupings of four long solid strips in each block reminded me of a group of candlesticks decorating a mantel. That's what inspired my original quilting design! I quilted a lighted candle in each solid strip, and then filled in the busier background areas with meander quilting.

DESIGN YOUR OWN

You can create your own Rocky Mountain Sparkler design. (Remember, they're half-dark/half-light blocks, so they can be used much like Log Cabin blocks.) Make exactly the size block you want by starting with the correct-sized squares, as given in the chart below.

Make intermediate-sized blocks (sizes that aren't listed) by varying all vertical seam allowances by 1/16". These simple blocks invite your creativity. Play with them awhile, and new uses for the Rocky Mountain Sparkler blocks will pop into your mind.

Rocky Mountain Sparkler blocks take on a different look when you cut the twin-triangle units into three equal pieces instead of four. Who's to say you must cut equal segments? Try experimenting with random cuts. Why arrange the slices in the shape of a mountain every time? No reason. Try mixing them up. You don't even have to stitch a perfect 45° angle every time. Cut across the two beginning squares at a different angle; then shuffle and repiece squares before making vertical slices. Changing the angle will change your whole perspective.

FINISHED BLOCKS	CUT 2 SQUARES	TWIN TRIANGLE UNITS	WIDTH OF SEGMENTS
6" x 9"	7" x 7"	6½" x 6½"	1⅝"
6½" x 10"	7½" x 7½"	7" x 7"	1¾"
7" x 11"	8" x 8"	7½" x 7½"	1⅞"
7½" x 12"	8½" x 8½"	8" x 8"	2"
8" x 13"	9" x 9"	8½" x 8½"	2⅛"
8½" x 14"	9½" x 9½"	9" x 9"	2¼"
9" x 15"	10" x 10"	9½" x 9½"	2⅜"
9½" x 16"	10½" x 10½"	10" x 10"	2½"
10" x 17"	11" x 11"	10½" x 10½"	2⅝"
10½" x 18"	11½" x 11½"	11" x 11"	2¾"

For Designing Minds

If you are an experienced quilter, no doubt your mind is full of questions and ideas by now. Some are logical extensions of the simplified procedures described in the project instructions. Others may have occurred to you as you studied the quilt photos in this book. Great designs are often born of simple questions like, "What if . . . ," so ask them. Challenge yourself to find the answers. Your best quilts are yet to be made! You have the power to work out the answers to any of your own questions by experimenting with scraps of fabric. It's always time well spent. To help you along, here are some easy ways to design your own variations of the quilts in this book.

- Choose as few as two contrasting fabrics or as many as you like. Begin as though you were making a charm quilt, with every square cut from a different fabric.

- Change the finished size and/or shape of the project by changing the number and/or placement of the squares in the beginning grid.

- Make your finished patchwork come out larger or smaller by changing the size of the beginning squares. Any size square will do. Exact finished measurements are difficult to predict, since they vary with the changing angles and with the width of the seam allowances. You can certainly make an educated guess, based on the projects in the book. I usually assume that the finished size of a quilt is the size it was meant to be. If I need to enlarge something to make it fit a particular bed or wall, I often add one or more pieced or plain borders.

- Customize your tracing guide to fit your needs. If you begin with larger or smaller squares than specified in one of the projects, you will need a different-sized tracing guide. You can make a custom-fitted tracing guide for any project by enlarging or shrinking any of the diagrams in this book. Remember that the AB line must match the finished width of your grid squares.

Note: If you change the width of the beginning squares, you will also need to change the width of the background strips that are sewn around the grid. They are cut half as wide as the cut measurement of the squares, plus ½" for seam allowances. For example, for squares cut 6" x 6", cut the background strips 3½" wide.

- Create a new and original design just by changing the angle of the two crossed lines on the tracing guide. A small change in the angle will result in a new look, so go for it!

The tracing-guide diagrams with the individual projects will not help if you use a different angle, but it is simple to make the one you need. Draft your own tracing-guide diagram by first drawing the crossed lines at the angle of your choice and then drawing a box around them, with the intersection of the angled lines at the center of the box. Make the box the exact correct size for the project's tracing guide by making sure that the crossed lines within it (segments AB) are the same length as the finished width of your grid squares.

I hope that you will be able to use some of these ideas in your own work. Just remember that these techniques are simply meant to put some fun into your quilting. Never take yourself or your quilting too seriously. Enjoy it for a lifetime.

Meet the Author

Martha Thompson has a knack for geometry and a love of color and texture. It's no wonder that patchwork quilts became her favorite form of self-expression about 18 years ago. She lives near Seattle, Washington, with her husband of 33 years. Two sons, one daughter-in-law, and one precious granddaughter make up her family.

Martha enjoys friendships, walking, yoga, cooking, reading, and travel. She feels very fortunate in being able to spend much of her time in volunteer work with AIDS care teams. She leads the Stone Soup Quilting Ministry through the annual production of 150 large quilts for adult cancer patients of Fred Hutchinson Cancer Research Center in Seattle.

Dozens of volunteers, each with her own poignant cancer story, find comfort for themselves as they work on these lovely quilts for the comfort of strangers. Martha also enjoys teaching and encouraging other quilters.